Discovering the Other

Discovering the Other

Asset-Based Approaches to Building Community Together

CAMERON HARDER

ALBAN

Alban Institute
Herndon, VA
www.alban.org

The Alban Institute

2121 Cooperative Way, Suite 100

Herndon, VA 20171

Unless otherwise noted, all Scripture quotations are from the New Revised Standard Version of the Bible, copyright © 1989, Division of Christian Education of the National Council of the Churches of Christ in the United States of America, and are used by permission.

Library of Congress Cataloging-in-Publication Data

Harder, Cam, 1954-
 Discovering the other : asset-based approaches to building community together / Cameron Harder.
   p. cm.
 Includes bibliographical references (p. 185).
 ISBN 978-1-56699-429-3
 1. Communities--Religious aspects--Christianity. 2. Church. I. Title.
 BV625.H37 2013
 253--dc23
                          2012023980

13   14   15   16   17   VP   5   4   3   2   1

Contents

127957

Preface

One fall CiRCLe M (Centre for Rural Community Leadership and Ministry), a nonprofit I direct, organized a conference on the church and community development. In workshops, worship, and conversation, one church leader after another shared stories of how their congregations had cared for their communities, how they provided relief after fire and flood, supported grieving families, looked after youth and elders in the community, stepped into gaps in community health care, and much more. After the conference one participant who hadn't been involved in church conferences before said, "I had no idea pastors and churches are doing so much good in their communities. I think the general perception is that they are just out there trying to push their ideology on people and get them to join their church."

The truth is that all across our countries in thousands of small ways, faith groups are daily offering hope and care to their neighborhoods. But very few of these acts get public recognition; the *sins* of the church seem to make much better press than its acts of kindness. We will look at reasons for that in chapter 2. However, the sometimes prurient interests of the press notwithstanding, I think it is fair to say that the PR problem is at least in part the church's own making.

I've noticed that a centripetal force, a kind of gravity, operates in church life that pulls Christians toward a temporal and geographic center. In my experience, that gravity includes a need to be with like-minded people, a desire for Christian friendship, a shared organizational history, the comfortable habit of regular worship, the joy of participating in corporate liturgy, a desire to access the skills of clergy or to please clergy, the need to organize maintenance for the physical church building, and so on. This centering force is a wonderful thing; without it, people of faith would drift away from each other. However, unchecked, the "gravity" can create problems.

Gravity may center a congregation in *time*. I did a study of congregations in Toronto and discovered that each had a honeymoon period. The churches looked back to a favorite pastor, a time of growth or active young families—a golden age. The stories most often repeated were drawn from that golden period.

Of course, all Christians center themselves on stories: the story of Israel, Jesus, and the church; the stories of their own personal and congregational origins. But sometimes more energy is spent hoarding, protecting, and polishing these gems of the past than spending them on new possibilities for the future. This is particularly the case when the golden age becomes the standard by which all later ministry is assessed. As golden age stories gain glory in their retelling, it becomes less and less likely that any present ministry can measure up to the heroic efforts of the past. The result is that congregations can live with a chronic sense of loss and low self-esteem.

There is also a centripetal tendency for a congregation to center itself in *space,* to pull in toward the church building rather than pushing (and accompanying) its members out into the community. After years of watching this happen in large congregations that I pastored, I began to feel that I was the chief operator of a giant vacuum, working diligently to suck the people and resources of our community into the programs and pews of our church.

In a small effort to reverse the suction, to breathe *out,* I started a group called "Faith Works." I wanted to gather folks in their work sites to reflect on what God was up to in those places. We loosely used some fine material from the Lutheran Church in America called *Connections: Faith and World* by Norma Cook Everist and Nelvin Vos as a guide for conversation.[1]

The initial meeting changed my perspective. I asked, "Who wants to be first to take us through their workplace?" A young woman put up her hand. "Where do you work?" I asked. She said she was a massage therapist. I was a bit taken aback. Never having had a massage, I harbored some unfortunate stereotypes about it. And one of our group was a distinguished retired pastor. I wondered whether he would regard a massage clinic (I was thinking "parlor") as an appropriate place to begin our exploration of faith and work.

But the woman was keen, so off we went. She showed us her worktable, oils, and techniques and told us what it was like to give a massage. Then we sat down in the waiting room to think about how our faith connected to her work. No one spoke for several long moments. Then finally the retired pastor looked at the therapist and said with some intensity, "I think your calling is much like mine. You're offering a physical form of confession and absolution. People come in here with knots in their bodies from all of the stresses and problems of their life. And they expose their bodies to you and allow you to touch those knots. It often hurts. You said sometimes there are tears—both from the physical sensation and from talking about what has created the tension. You accept them. You physically release the tension. You bless their bodies with your hands. And they go back out into the world with a new sense of grace and freedom." The therapist listened to the old pastor with tears in her eyes and said, "I will never think of my work the same way again." And, deeply humbled, neither did I.

Similar experiences occurred again and again as we visited each other's workplaces. Essentially we were doing a faith form of appreciative inquiry, though I didn't know that language then. We were discovering that God is active in the 99 percent of people's lives that are lived outside the church, and we were naming, celebrating, and trying to faithfully interpret that divine activity.

When churches take seriously life *outside* their buildings and their Sunday morning sacred time, they give their communities an inexpressible gift. Weekday life tends to be filled with routines: getting children ready for school; braving heat, cold, or traffic to get to work; moving paper, hammering nails, applying bandages, doing whatever the work requires just as one has for years; coming home to make meals, watch TV, sleep, and start all over. Ordinary life can feel flat and featureless.

Yet we humans want to feel that our lives are meaningful. In Gregory Pierce's anthology of workplace theology, *Of Human Hands,* Hal Miller claims that we are "transcendence junkies."[2] We want to know that what we do *matters.* Studies of happiness around the world show that people have a much greater sense of well-being when they can see a clear purpose to their lives.[3] Unfortunately, we tend to look for transcendent meaning in the brief and exceptional rather than in the ordinary moments of life.

The church can fall into this trap too if it testifies only to stories of great failure and rescue. But churches transform the spirit of their communities when they help them see, beneath their pavement, pastures, and office panels, the divine mystery, the triune God at work. The tools in this book help congregations see that all of life is saturated by the sacred and give them energy to begin living as if it were so.

Perhaps that alone, though, would not be sufficient reason for writing, since many good resources on community-building tools have already been published. But this book looks for God not only *through* the lens of such tools but also *in* the tools themselves. It is an effort to understand how processes like appreciative inquiry and asset mapping reflect the character and community-building style of the God whom Christians worship as divine community.

Acknowledgments

First, I want to acknowledge my dear Dorothy, who has borne the cross of being married to a pastor and theologian for thirty-seven years (and counting), but who, from the beginning, reminded me—and modeled for me—the truth that most of our ministry happens outside the church.

I am indebted to my seminary students who used these tools in their field education programs and provided most of the on-the-ground wisdom you might find in this book.

I am also very appreciative of my editor, Beth Gaede, for her longsuffering patience in waiting for this book through its many stops and starts.

Finally, I deeply appreciate the hundreds of churches and communities in Canada, the United States, the United Kingdom, and India who hospitably welcomed me and offered me a glimpse into what it is that helps them live with faith and hope.

Chapter 1

The Church's Community-Building Mission

In 2004 I spent several weeks visiting villages in rural India. One of them was a few hours south of Kolkata in northeastern India. I was poled across a lazy river while standing on a two-foot-wide boat, then bounced on the back of a bicycle cart along a narrow, cobbled path that ran between neat squares of rice paddy and banana trees until we came to the village. It was a cluster of airy, mud-walled homes thatched with rice straw. Drying patties of cow dung polka-dotted the sides of houses. The whole village came out to greet me, men in white shirts and pants, women in colorful sarees. They pressed me with flower bouquets and offered green coconut milk to drink. It seemed like a place of lovely simplicity.

But the reality was somewhat darker. For an hour or so they told me of their struggles with hunger and illness. For decades they had lived with virtually no food three months out of each year. Their children were victims of chronic dysentery and diarrhea. There was a high rate of miscarriage. Women were confined to their homes by cultural and religious tradition. They were lonely and illiterate.

During the previous year, however, with the encouragement of Lutheran World Service India, a nongovernmental organization (NGO), they had taken enormous strides toward healthy living. The villagers had formed a grain bank, contributing after the harvests and borrowing when the food ran out. They had drilled a well that gave potable water and no longer drank from the village ponds that were used for animal watering and sanitation. The women had formed a self-help group to share ideas about child care. They had even driven out of town the liquor vendor who kept many of their men chronically drunk. In a short period of time they had made remarkable, sustainable gains in well-being.

At the end of my visit, I asked them, "In this year of amazing changes, what is the best thing that happened for you?" I assumed that they would identify one of the economic or health benefits. They thought for a bit and finally one woman stood up. She said, "The best thing is that we have found each other." And they all nodded.

Food, health, literacy. All good things. But those villagers had discovered that these good things simply supported their capacity to fully enjoy each other. For them, *finding each other* was the point of it all.

THE PURPOSE OF THIS BOOK

In the end, that is the purpose of this book: to help you find each other—the other in the congregation and the other in the community. The tools described here will most likely lead you into programs and projects that will enrich your congregation's mission. But most important, in the process they will engage you with others, with their stories, their hopes, their gifts. And in the end that's really what all the programs are aimed at anyway. We're out to *build community*.

The process of building community is like a treasure hunt—it's about *discovering* each other. It's a challenge because many things keep us hidden, disconnected from one another. The climate keeps us indoors in hot southern summers and cold northern winters. Geography isolates. Social status brings us into contact with some people but keeps us apart from others. Even things we value greatly as congregations can isolate us. Our buildings can become religious ghettos as the energy for outreach is absorbed in feeding the church building's survival needs.

Of course internal squabbles or declining membership can turn a congregation in on itself. Martin Luther says that this being curved in on ourselves is the definition of sin. Certainly, it dramatically reduces our connections with people outside the church. But it also weakens internal bonds. If Redeemer Church's interest is mostly in Redeemer Church, then holding Redeemer together becomes its primary mission. Conflict threatens that unity. To avoid conflict, people avoid engaging each other at a deep level.

DISCOVERING THE OTHER TAKES RESEARCH

The first move in building community then must be to increase our awareness of each other. We have to *hunt* for each other, do some *research*, start *listening*. Community begins when people *seek* to know each other. Remember that old song "Getting to know you, getting to know all about you"? That's the first step in the love that binds us together.

From the beginning the Bible talks about love as *knowing*: Genesis 4:1 says, "Now the man *knew* his wife Eve, and she conceived and bore Cain" (italics mine). Love and knowledge also depend on each other in our relationship to God. We read in 1 John 4:8, "Whoever does not love does not know God, for God is love." In the great love chapter, 1 Corinthians 13, Paul sees love's culmination this way: "I will know fully, even as I have been fully known" (v. 12).

Knowing each other doesn't come automatically. It takes *courage*. What we find out about the other (and they about us) may be hard to handle. It takes intentional action, *seeking* the other. It takes *discipline*—focused time set apart to listen to each other, to unwrap our hearts. Churches that have life-transforming ministries are churches that structure opportunities for people to know each other and to know their communities. Simply sitting beside each other in the pew on Sunday or working side by side on Monday doesn't do it. Bethania Lutheran has a potluck every Sunday after church. They laugh, listen, tell stories, share their lives. The men of my own congregation meet at a restaurant *every* Friday morning of the year at 7:00 just to talk and get to know each other. Building community means making time to hear each other's stories.

This book is an introduction to some tools for seeking and knowing each other that church and community builders have found helpful. The tools all owe a debt to the community-based participatory research movement that grew out of the work of Paulo Freire, a Latin American educator. He saw that if only a few are allowed to define the community publicly, if they are the only true "knowers" of the community, relationships will not be loving but oppressive. In his experience communities began to pull out of poverty and oppression when they drew their self-image from the people as a whole rather than an elite few.[1]

Most of the time, however, communities come to know themselves through the eyes of powerful leaders, in much the same way that women have historically tended to see themselves through the eyes of male interpreters. The sources of knowledge, the textbooks, tend to be written by people who don't share the people's struggles and in fact often contribute to them. The knowledge the people gain from such elites tends to reinforce their sense of themselves as a people without resources, reliant on others, helpless and hopeless. This was the sad legacy of the residential schools in Canada that sought to reorient the self-understanding of its aboriginal peoples.

It happens in congregations too. The pastor hears everyone's stories, but the people hear few of each other's. The pastor distills the congregation's identity from the stories and tells the people who they are. But they are left unable to do that for themselves— like baby birds dependent on regurgitation from their mother's beak. That arrangement gives the pastor a great deal of power and status. It forms a community gathered around a minister, but it doesn't form a ministering community deeply connected to each other and to God.

However, when people are equipped to hear each other's stories, marvelous things can happen. In my first parish my colleague invited a group of people from Lutheran Lay Renewal to come and tell their "God stories." This is a group of laity who are willing to travel at their own expense from various places in North America to put on renewal weekends in host congregations. Their stories were honest and interesting. But what they did afterward transformed our church culture. They divided the congregational members who had come to listen into groups of five or six. Group members were asked to share with each other answers to some simple questions: When did God first become more than a word to you? When have you felt a sense of wonder? Tell about a time recently when you felt that you were interacting with God. Our people, who had known each other in some cases for many years, were astonished as they listened to these stories of faith discovery. Hearing that God was present in the mundane reality of their neighbors enabled them to recognize God's activity in their own lives and tell about it to others.

The delight to us as pastors was that after years of trying unsuccessfully to get small group Bible studies going, more than half a dozen groups formed spontaneously in the wake of this event. People were hungry to know each other and amazed to realize that God was at work in their lives.

Another example: At the conclusion of our congregation's confirmation program, we help our students think through the experience of God and community in their preschool, elementary school, and adolescent lives. We encourage them to write honestly about their faith, their unanswered questions, their difficult and defining experiences. Each confirmand reads his or her story at a supper at which parents and baptismal sponsors are present. The gathering is always profoundly moving. There are lots of tears. Parents often have never really heard the "God thoughts" of their own children. They are astonished at how family traditions and tragedies have shaped their children's faith.

INTRODUCTION TO THE TOOLS

The power of people sharing their stories with each other is at the heart of community-based research. It is an intentional process for helping people to get to know each other deeply, for building community. A pastor or trained leader, even an outside professor or consultant, helps a congregation put together a series of listening and sharing experiences with people from the community. Deeper relationships are formed in the process. And almost inevitably the experience leads to new directions for ministries that also build community.

Two tools for community-building ministry are described in this book: appreciative inquiry and asset mapping. They have been around for many years in community development circles. I discovered them on a sabbatical, while visiting communities in India, Canada, the United States, and the United Kingdom. I was looking for ways to help revitalize the congregations of western Canada that are served by students of the seminary where I teach and to get these leaders and congregations more deeply engaged with their communities.

Our seminary first used these tools with four small rural churches clustered around a larger town congregation. There were some struggles. At one point the rural churches had shared a pastor with the town congregation, but they split from the town church over a dispute regarding the pastor. Membership was declining in three of the rural churches. For these congregations, the future seemed bleak. They wanted to know where their members had all gone and whether there was any chance of getting them back.

I said that I would train a student to work with all five congregations, but I asked if they would take the student on as an intern. That way the student could live with them and really get to know them, and the student would have enough time to help them learn how to gather that information for themselves. They agreed. That step in itself required a cooperation between the rural and town points that began to rebuild communication.

The intern worked with a group of parish leaders to set up a series of interviews with both active and inactive members. These interviews were intended to help identify some of the congregations' concerns. Initially the process met with some resistance. Some were worried that congregational leaders were just looking for reasons to close the small churches down. But gradually people opened up. As they did, their responses were collated by the parish councils.

What came out of those interviews were many expressions of frustration. Young people were being excluded. Older people felt that worship was not connected to their economic realities. There was a sense of lost purpose.

The self-perception that emerged was quite negative. It was obvious that the congregations saw themselves as "problem places"—problems with youth, problems with attendance, problems with commitment.

So the intern organized a series of focus groups within each of the congregations. But instead of asking, "What's wrong?" he asked, "What's right?" which is the central question in a conversation method called *appreciative inquiry*, developed by David Cooperrider and Suresh Srivastva, professors of organizational behavior and development. We'll look at this process in more detail in chapter 3. Briefly, Cooperrider and Srivastva's assumption is that organizations change in the direction of their most frequently asked questions. Positive questions (such as "What's working?") create positive change; negative questions (such as "What's wrong?") generate blaming and discouragement.

The intern asked the focus group to discuss questions like these:

- What has been the highlight of your experience with this congregation?
- What are some of the things we do well?
- What have we done in the past that has really worked with youth?
- What do people really turn out for and why?
- What are three wishes that you have for this congregation?

The energy that developed in that parish was amazing to see. Self-esteem rose dramatically as they listened to each other's stories and discovered that they did some things very well. The positive discussion was a way of removing shame and restoring honor to the congregations.

The intern worked with a group to collate these responses. A second round of focus groups was held, but this time they were intercongregational. People were asked, "What resources do you have personally that we could bring to our future together?" The resources they were told to look for included personal experience, skills, hobbies, personality traits, congregational groups, things people owned, community connections, and so on.

Out of those gatherings came a growing sense that this was not a poor, dying parish but one rich in history, people, and resources. The job was to pull them together in creative ways—a form of asset mapping, which we will also explore further on in the book.

The internship ended while the parish was developing action plans, but the people had the process well in hand. They knew how to go back and repeat steps if they needed to. And they have moved forward in ministry with a new sense of purpose and God's presence.

When the people were asked what was the best thing that came out of that process of research, though, it was not a ministry program. They said what the Indian villagers had said: "We found each other. We reconnected with the folks from the town congregation. We've begun to feel like a whole community again." I believe they rediscovered their mission.

WHAT IS GOD REALLY UP TO?

The mission of the church has been imagined in a variety of ways. Constantine's goal was to erect a church building in every town. Missionaries sought to translate the Bible into every language, to baptize the masses, or to bring Christian "civilization" to the "heathen." Modern church growth fans want to fill every pew. Contemporary liturgists seek transcendent or contextually relevant worship services. And many congregants are satisfied as long as the church hangs around to baptize, marry, and bury them, and provide a bit of pastoral care and inspiration in between.

I believe that the church's mission is a subset of God's mission in the world. If that is the case, it follows that we need at least some sense of the direction in which God is going. Otherwise the church risks rowing against the divine current instead of with it.

What then is *God's* mission? Without presuming to understand the divine purpose for the whole universe, we might at least venture a classic answer in relation to humanity: "Well, to *save* us." Of course that begs the question "Save us from what?" Sin, death, and hell perhaps. But there must be more to God's mission than that. God can save us from all that bad stuff just by ending our existence—"Take away their breath . . . and [they] return to their dust," as the psalmist says (104:29).

Maybe instead of asking, "Saved *from* what?" we need to ask, "Saved *for* what?" After all, if *hope* is one of the definitive and lasting qualities of Christian life, as Paul suggests in 1 Corinthians 13, then it is worth asking not just "What do we fear or flee from?" but also "What kind of future do we hope for?"

Here are a few suggestive biblical passages. In 1 Corinthians 15:28 Paul says that God's desire is that ultimately "God may be all in all." Isaiah (11:9) looks forward to the day when the "earth will be full of the knowledge of the LORD as the waters cover the sea." The writer of Hebrews also hopes for the day when "they shall all know me [the Lord], from the least of them to the greatest" (8:11). Such passages suggest that God's mission ultimately is to saturate all of creation with God's own life.

And that Divine Life we will share is not solitary or self-focused. It has a communal shape. God intends, it seems, to embrace all creation within the fellowship of the Three. Revelation 21 describes it this way: "See, the home of God is among mortals. [God] will *dwell with them*; they will be [God's] peoples, and God . . . *will be with them*" (v. 3, italics mine). Jesus prays for that day to come in John 17:21: "As you, Father, are in me and I am in you, may they also be in us, so that the world may believe that you have sent me."

That divine-human dwelling will be reflected in a deep intra-human sharing of life and gifts. We read, "People will bring into it [the New Jerusalem] the glory and the honor of the nations" (Rev. 21:26).

The communal life of God is extended to relationships with, and within, nonhuman creation as well. In compelling imagery, Isaiah 11 looks forward to that all-embracing fellowship: "The wolf shall live with the lamb . . . the calf and the lion and the fatling together, and a little child shall lead them. . . . The nursing child shall play over the hole of the asp, and . . . the earth will be full of the knowledge of the LORD as the waters cover the sea" (vv. 6–9).

Simply put, can we say that God's mission is to *form communities that reflect and embody the life of the Trinity?*

That way of describing the mission of God makes sense when one looks at the structure of creation. Scientists tell us that, from smallest to largest, the universe appears to be a fractal collection of communities (through about fifty powers of ten increasing in size). Vibrating strings of energy form communities called quarks. Quarks of various kinds (up, down, strange, and so forth) form communities of protons, neutrons, electrons, and the like. They in turn form communities we call atoms, and those gather into various kinds of molecules. Communities of molecules form organelles, and those form cells. Trillions of cells form organisms like us, and this whole earthly biosphere of organisms and inorganics makes up a planet. Planets and suns form solar systems. And solar systems gather in galaxies, and the galaxies in clusters and the clusters in *super*clusters. And all through the universe run vast streams of warm-hot gas that feed and flow out of those galaxies, knitting the whole universe into one great, integrated community.

Even we humans, who consider ourselves individuals, are in fact a living community. In a *Discover* article, respected science writer Michael Tennesen tells about the work of medical researchers at Duke University who are studying the human *microbiome*—that enormous population of bacteria, fungi, viruses, and other microbes that live in the human body. They have found that there are twenty times as many of these microbes as there are cells in the body, up to two hundred trillion in an adult, and each of us hosts at least one thousand different species. Most are not parasites but form essential elements of human digestion, metabolism, and defense. Michael's conclusion: "Seen through the prism of the microbiome, a person is not so much an individual human body as a superorganism made up of diverse ecosystems, each teeming with microscopic creatures that are essential to our well-being."[2]

So, if God *is* community, if God has given a communal structure to the universe, and if God is leading humanity toward community that better reflects the character of God's own life, what does that suggest about God's attitude toward the communities in which our churches are located? Listen to these promises:

- "I know the plans I have for you [Israel], . . . plans for your welfare and not for harm, to give you a future with hope" (Jer. 29:11).
- "As the bridegroom rejoices over the bride, so shall your God rejoice over you, . . . O Jerusalem" (Isa. 62:5).
- "God is in the midst of the city; it shall not be moved; God will help it when the morning dawns" (Ps. 46:5).
- "But now thus says the LORD, he who created you, O Jacob, he who formed you, O Israel: Do not fear, for I have redeemed you; I have called you by name, you are mine. When you pass through the waters, I will be with you; and through the rivers, they shall not overwhelm you. . . . For I am the LORD your God, the Holy One of Israel, your Savior. . . . *You are precious in my sight, and honored, and I love you*" (Isa. 43:1–4, italics mine).

The first thing to notice is that these promises—like most in the Bible—were given not to human individuals but to *collective* entities—to Israel, to Jerusalem, to the Hebrew people, to the church. And even promises given to individuals often had a community in mind: Abraham and Sarah are promised descendants so that all the nations of the earth will be blessed (Gen. 22:18). Isaac blesses Jacob in Genesis 28:3 not for Jacob's own sake but for the sake of communities to come: "May God Almighty bless you and make you fruitful and increase your numbers until you become a *community of peoples*" (NIV, italics mine).

Second, and even more important, hear the deep affection, the love, expressed in those verses. Clearly, God *loves communities and saves communities.* Christians have tended to appropriate those promises for themselves *personally,* as if God relates to us primarily as individuals. But if God is community and the universe is community from the bottom up, then it makes sense that God loves communities at all sizes. God loves not just human beings but also the towns we live in, the earth's biosphere, and beyond.

So God's mission is not simply to pluck souls out of the fires of hell one by one. God saves us *for* community—to *be* community. God saves us *by* the healing, faith-building work *of* communities, *in* communities.

And who will tell our communities that, if not the church? Who will tell the farms, the towns and cities devastated this year by earthquake, hurricane, tornado, flood, and fire that—against all evidence to the contrary—they have *not* been abandoned by God? Who will say, "When you pass through the waters, I will be with you; and through the rivers, they shall not overwhelm you. . . . For I am . . . your Savior. . . . You are precious in my sight, and honored, and I love you" (Isa. 43:1–4)?

If God's mission is to *build* communities that reflect the quality of life shared by Father, Son, and Spirit, then the church must find its own calling within that divine impulse.

THE TROUBLE WITH THE TRINITY AS MODEL FOR HUMAN COMMUNITY

Unfortunately, if you listen to our God language, God's communal interest isn't obvious. Think about the last time you heard God mentioned outside of church (not in profanity). If you are Canadian, you may have trouble remembering such a time, because we're not really fond of public theological conversation. In fact, in some public occupations (such as government jobs), talking about one's faith is illegal. But assuming there's been such an occasion, how was God *named* in it?

Most likely you didn't hear the name into which we are baptized—"Father, Son, and Holy Spirit." In my experience Canadians and Americans generally refer almost exclusively to God as "God" or "Lord," or make some vague reference to "help from above." I've rarely heard the name of the Three used outside of church liturgies.

Yet that three-person name was the family name we were given at our baptism. It's strange that we so blithely drop it. In the classic Christian creeds, we claim to believe in a God who is three persons in one being. Yet our operational theology is not particularly trinitarian. Certainly that messy, mysterious business about the threeness of God floats about in the background somewhere. But our actual God talk refers almost exclusively to God's oneness. When we do speak of God in more personal terms, we seem to prefer to focus on one of the Three ("Father," "Spirit," "Jesus") at a time, keeping our reference unitary rather than trinitarian.

On the rare occasions when we speak about God as Trinity ("Trinity Sunday" in my tradition), we usually start with God's oneness and then differentiate. We imagine one substance appearing in different forms. We imagine God as a tree trunk with three branches, or an actor playing three different roles, or water in its triple state as ice, liquid, and steam. *Essentially* one, secondarily three.

The Seductive Power of Monotheistic Language

The truth is, we Canadians and Americans are monotheists at heart—and that's understandable. Monotheism makes things simple. In our multifaith societies it's a lot easier to relate to Muslim, Hindu, Jew, Buddhist, and "nonspecified other" believers if we all talk about God rather than Allah, Ganesh, Yahweh, Jesus, Buddha, or Gaia. Well-meaning people of all faiths are looking for common ground. It's nice to think that we're all talking about the same thing if we only speak about "God."

That's an illusion though, as I discovered in India. India is a very religious country; people love to talk theology. Gods are everywhere. The welcome sign in the New Delhi airport says, "In India there are over 360 million gods—there should be one for you." Gods are perched on the dashboards of taxis, standing in airports, clustered in rural courtyards, painted on walls. You can't avoid talking about god(s). But listening to Indian taxi drivers, farmers, and scientists, I realized that Hindu conceptions of divinity really are quite different from those of historic Christianity. Hindu's ultimate reality (Brahman) turns a karmic wheel that binds all people to a rigid system of cause and effect. The poor and the untouchable are simply living out the unavoidable effects of their own and their ancestors' sins. Belief in that sort of god has formed a highly stratified community.

The God whom we see in Jesus, who lives with and becomes one of the cursed untouchables, is very different. This God is characterized by a grace that frees us from the prison of past acts for new life and a different kind of community.

So when Christians and Hindus refer to "God," they are *not* always talking about the same person. Names, personalities, *style*, and *goals* are essential to what it means to be a person. When the core characteristics of our gods are radically different, using the same generic name for them is not helpful.

Yet monotheistic language persists. Perhaps that's because it conforms so nicely to our dominant social structures.[3] These are usually pyramids. Globe-straddling corporations, like Microsoft, have that triangular shape: there are many computer users and code writers on the bottom, Bill Gates on top. Until recently most of the world's major political systems were also designed as pyramids, with many people on the bottom, a few nobles higher up, and a monarch on top. Even now our democratically elected governments retain a fair bit of pyramid power. We have the option of choosing our rulers from time to time, but the power is still concentrated at the top.

Pyramids as a way to structure an organization are popular. Those on top like a pyramidal structure because they are supported by many people. They get fame, power, and usually a fair bit of wealth. Those underneath like to have someone looking after them, making the big decisions. It's nice to be children, with a father or mother in Ottawa or Washington looking after us. We have less responsibility. Even in the church, that has been our model: one pastor in charge, one flock depending on him or her. If the flock gets too big for one pastor, then we may have several, but there still has to be someone at the top. And over it all is one God.

We like pyramids. They seem stable, reliable. But I was on the bottom of a human pyramid once—in my grade ten gym class— and it didn't feel very stable to me. I had two big guys with bad BO and bony knees digging into my back, and there were three layers above me. We poor folks at the bottom had to bear the weight of everyone on top. It wasn't long before my legs gave out and my nose was flattened against the gym floor. My experience of pyramids is that they tend to crush the people on the bottom.

More seriously, when we speak about our relationship to God in a pyramidal, monotheistic fashion, we imply that a huge gap exists between us and God. God is on the top, most are on the bottom, and various levels of more or less pious, just, or successful folks are in between. In fact, that's pretty much how the ancient heresy, Gnosticism, imagines our relationship to God. God is the Great and Wholly Other who can't get the divine hands dirty by direct contact with us. So God's presence is conveyed to us through layers of intermediaries who are more worthy of being in the presence of God than we are. We experience this God at the top as unapproachable, excluding sinful human beings from the divine presence, even violently.

Jesus turns this image of God upside down. Here was one in whom people experienced the reign of God—healing, new hope, forgiveness, food and wine in abundance. They were transformed people. And yet the God they met in Christ was nothing like a monarch perched on a pyramid. Jesus came into the world near the bottom and worked his way down. He was born homeless and had become a refugee in Egypt by the age of two. He became an itinerant preacher as an adult, lived on welfare provided by women, got into trouble with the church and the law, and was eventually executed for treason, blasphemy, and making "terrorist" threats. In almost every society I know, folks like that would be bottom-feeders, losers. And so it would have been assumed of Jesus, except that God raised Jesus from the dead, glorified, declaring him to be the Son of God.

"Surprise!" should be our Easter greeting. Surprise, because we find God not at the top but on the bottom. We find God stooped down, washing the dirty feet of friends. Looking up, bare-chested, with a towel over his shoulder, Jesus says, "If I, your Lord and Teacher, have washed your feet, you also ought to wash one another's feet" (John 13:14). This one, Paul says, did not count equality with God a thing to reach for, to cling to—but emptied himself, taking the form of a slave, becoming subject even to death, as Paul says in Philippians 2. When Jesus's friends quarrel about who will sit next to him at the top of the pyramid, Jesus says, "The Son of Man came not to be served but to serve" (Matt. 20:28; Mark 10:45). To be with Jesus, to be close to God, is to be with the people. In a pyramid, that would be at the bottom.

But the writer of 1 Peter deconstructs that triangular image completely when he calls us *all* a "royal priesthood" (2:9)! If *all* are royalty, what does that do to the pyramid? It flattens it, just like the one in my gym class. There's no ladder left to climb.

So, what if we imagined God surrounding and among, rather than above the people? What if we were to begin not with God's unity but God's *comm*unity, God's diversity?

That's where the early church began—with the experience of threeness. Many of the first Christians had grown up with the confession "Yahweh, our God, is one God." But the *experience* of God that the disciples had in the life and ministry of Jesus was diverse. They sensed the Divine in Jesus himself. They heard Jesus's promise of the Advocate, the Holy Spirit who would empower them for witness in the world, stand by them in times of distress, and lead them into the truth. And they heard Jesus talk to the Father as "Abba"—that is, "Daddy." What was the relationship between these three? That was the puzzle that occupied the early church. It's never been solved in some simple, analytic way. But out of the early Christians' reflection has come an understanding of God as deeply integrated community that also changed their view of *human* life.

God Is Holy—We Are Not

It is not enough, however, simply to assert, "Because God is and loves community, we should be more community minded." Obviously, communities as such are not always a good thing. They can be oppressive. Sometimes in families, urban board rooms, or rural towns, people are pigeonholed. They are unable to grow or change because they are pinned in place by the perceptions and expectations of those close to them. A few people may hold most of the power. The truth is, in every community, wherever human beings are close and vulnerable to each other, there seems to be some sin and suffering.

So it's not enough to give congregations tools for community building. Compare community building to home building: we need tools to build the house, but we also need skills for using them, and we need some understanding of basic principles of construction and design. What *sort* of house will serve its inhabitants well and stand up over time? Further on, this book will introduce you to the tools for community building and some step-by-step approaches to using them (skill development). But first we need to ask, "What *sort* of community will serve us well? What are God's community-building principles?"

One option is to model our communities on the relationships between Father, Son, and Spirit. This theological move—often called the "social doctrine of the Trinity"—has a long history in the Eastern church, beginning with the Cappadocians, who were fourth-century monastics and scholars. It has been much less popular in Western Christian traditions that are more dependent on Augustine. Augustine followed the Greeks, who regarded God's oneness, God's ultimate simplicity, as the most important aspect of divine reality.

We could retrieve the social doctrine of the Trinity from the Eastern church. But to use the Trinity as a blueprint for human interactions requires an assumption that shouldn't come easily for us. "God is God, we are not," we say. So several questions arise: What makes us think that our messy, sinful churches could relate in ways that are anything like the relationships between Father, Son, and Holy Spirit? Second, even if there is a valid correspondence between God's life and ours, how do we know what God's internal life is like? Do we really have *access* to the dynamics of inner trinitarian life, or is it hidden from us? And finally, *if* God's life offers a useful guide to our own community building, how do we *read* or describe the dynamics of that life in a way that makes them useful for shaping a congregation's ministry? In appreciative inquiry, for example, we ask, "What has been working?" Theologically we mean, "How has God been at work among us?" It is possible to answer that question only if we have a sense of God's *style*—how God's life intersects with ours—and if we can compare that style to what we see happening.

Let's begin with the first question: can we really infer from God's life to ours? What makes us think that the Creator's life is anything like the creatures'? Even if there is a deep relationship between the two, they can be quite dissimilar. One doesn't *have* to be a reflection of the other. For example, the church has attempted to describe the relationships between Father, Son, and Spirit using words like *begetting, proceeding,* and *glorifying.* But that's definitely not the sort of language one might use to describe Bob and Mary's relationship to Kathy and John in the young parents' group at church.

Yet the Bible suggests that it *is* possible for human community to genuinely reflect the life of God. Luther understood that God creates "from nothing"—meaning that all things find their existence in God. If this is so, one would expect the life of God to be stamped in some way on God's handiwork. Several New Testament writers hint at this in their description of Christ's relationship to creation: "All things came into being through him, and without him not one thing came into being" (John 1:3); "all things have been created through him and for him . . . and in him all things hold together" (Col. 1:16–17); "in these last days he has spoken to us by a Son, whom he appointed heir of all things, through whom he also created the worlds. He is the reflection of God's glory and the exact imprint of God's very being, and he sustains all things by his powerful word" (Heb. 1:2–3). Without spelling it out, these verses imply that in a very intimate way, Christ, in union with the work of the Father and the Spirit, gives shape to all creation.

But more than that, in Genesis 1:26 God says, "Let us make humankind *in our image,* according to our likeness" (italics mine). Influential Yale theologian Miroslav Volf, in *After Our Likeness,* says that one can't escape the Bible's assertion that human communities are created to correspond in some way to the life of the Trinity. He points out, however, that this correspondence can only be a limited one. Individually we are not—we cannot be—immortal, omniscient, holy beings in the way that the Trinity is; our communities are even less so at times. Therefore the patterning, we must keep in mind, can only be faint and analogous—like a schoolchild trying to draw Michelangelo's *David* on a scrap of paper with a crayon. Still, it suggests that when we look at humanity (and perhaps *all* creation, for the "made in our image" statement doesn't have to be exclusive to humans), we do see *something* of God.

Perhaps a useful metaphor is that of a child in her mother's womb. German theologian Jürgen Moltmann speaks of creation "in" God (pan-*en*-theism). Lutheran theologian Robert Jensen talks about the "roominess" of God. If God is three, there is space between the persons—room for us. The way in which human life interacts with that divine hospitality seems somewhat similar to the life within life that occurs in pregnancy.

A mother interacts with her unborn child in a variety of ways. She supplies the nourishment the child needs to live and grow. She surrounds, supports, succors the child. Her DNA sculpts the child's image. Her life flows through the placenta to the child. The child comes to know her voice, feels her movements. He is affected by the food she eats. And the child affects the mother, moving, kicking, stretching her, drawing on her resources.

This metaphor has its limits, naturally. But it helps us imagine God as deeply related to creation. The child is not the mother. But the child's life is affected by and patterned in certain ways on the mother's. Not everything that happens in the womb is the mother's doing. Yet the mother is involved with it all. Similarly God's life and ours are not identical. But perhaps we can fairly say that our lives are patterned on God's in some way.

Can We Really Know the Divine Community?

Even if in some way God's life corresponds to what ours should be, the second question I pose is how do we *find out* what the life of Father, Son, and Spirit is really like? Is it possible for us to know the inner working of the Trinity? It is my conviction that such knowledge is not only possible but necessary for Christian faith, following this line of reasoning:

1. All of creation is interconnected. One of Einstein's great contributions to modern science was his discovery (now experimentally verified) that the universe is made up of relationships. This is his general theory of relativity. It posits that space-time is not a container for all the stuff of the universe but a complex web of interactions. Gravity, electromagnetism, weak and strong nuclear forces bind the universe together across space. Cause and effect, history and hope bind it together across time. As a result each element in some way acts on every other. What affects one, affects the whole.
2. We believe that this interdependence has been created and is sustained by God.
3. If this is so, then all of creation is connected *to* God and connected to itself *through* God. God is intimately involved with the life and history of creation.
4. God took on an even deeper, more profound connection with creation in Jesus. Taking on human flesh, God's connection to creation becomes clearly visible to us. And because in Christ our human flesh has in turn been taken up into God, we get a glimpse of the relationships among Father, Son, and Spirit.

Because of creation and incarnation human (and nonhuman) history has become entwined with the relationships among the Three. As the Three interact with creation, they also interact with each other. The Father speaks to Jesus and to the crowds (John 12). Jesus breathes the Holy Spirit on his disciples (John 20). The disciples witness the interaction of Father, Son, and Spirit in Jesus's baptism at the Jordan (Luke 3). Hanging on the cross, publicly humiliated, Jesus cries out to the Father in the hearing of all, "My God, why have you forsaken me?" (Matt. 27:46).

To be a Christian is to believe that the history of Jesus truly reveals the inner history of God—that Jesus is not just a mask God wore for a moment and then cast aside. We believe that those who walked with Jesus were actually watching Father, Son, and Spirit interact with each other and with us. More than that, because we are connected to Christ (genetically, socially, historically), we have been drawn into that divine community. So we do have access to that life. That doesn't mean we can make absolute claims about God's inner life. We surely have had only the briefest glimpse. But it may be enough to help us shape our own lives.

Finally, if God's trinitarian life is, at least in some ways, the source and model for our human community, and if Jesus's life reveals that model to us, how then shall we read it? What does it look like? How can we describe it in a way that allows us to apply our community-building tools?

Clearly, the correspondence between God's life—as Christians understand it—and ours cannot be *structural*. For example, God is Three in One; we are billions. Each of the Three is everywhere present; we are individually confined to one place, physically separated from each other. Rather than structure, I think the correspondence has to do with *style*. We "read" the Trinity by observing the nature of the relationships among the Three as they are revealed in Jesus's life. On that basis I would suggest the following description of trinitarian relationships as principles for building human community.

Trinitarian Principles for Building Healthy Communities

The heart of Jesus's relationship with his Abba was an ongoing conversation that punctuated his days and occupied his nights. In the Gospels the key moments of revelation are often presented as a conversation between divine persons: "This is my Son, the Beloved" (Matt. 3:17); "'Father, glorify your name'. . . . 'I have glorified it, and I will glorify it again'" (John 12:28); "Father, hallowed be your name" (Luke 11:2); "Father, if it is possible, let this cup pass from me" (Matt. 26:39); "My God, why have you forsaken me?" (Matt. 27:46); "Father, into your hands I commend my spirit" (Luke 23:46). John devotes an entire chapter of his Gospel— chapter 17—to Jesus's conversation with the Father immediately before Jesus is betrayed by those for whom he has been praying. In the Gospels Divine Love notices and listens. Love speaks out of a desire to share One's heart honestly and respond to the heart of the Other. Love is deep communication that allows One to take the Other fully into account. Conversation appears to be central to the loving relationships within God.

Community Is Built Out of Conversation

The Trinity appears to relate in the same way to us—through conversation. The Bible and much of Christian theology use communication-oriented terms to describe that relationship. Genesis 1 ("Let *us* make") implies that creation takes place in the midst of a divine council. (Apparently we are the product of a committee!) God's *promises*, from Abraham through Moses and the prophets, are the basis of Israel's hope and God's *warnings* are the source of their resistance and repentance. The conversation continues throughout the New Testament until the words of the risen Christ to the seven churches in Revelation, and our final cry, "*Marantha!* Come, Lord Jesus!"

Central to this eon-spanning conversation is Jesus, the Word who creates and who becomes creation: "In the beginning was the Word. . . . All things came into being through him. . . . And the Word became flesh" (John 1:1–3, 14). From the earliest days Christians have understood this to mean that in becoming flesh, Christ the Word became connected to all human communities, and indeed, all of creation. Luther described this understanding of enfleshment, or incarnation, as God being "clothed" in creation. The term is useful because it means, on the one hand, that the Word is concealed. When one looks at human communities that have struggled and suffered so intensely over their histories, it is not obvious that the Word that sustains them is a word of *Love*. Yet, when one listens closely and appreciatively, the strong refrain of Love's song can be heard sustaining, making new.

If God is clothed in creation, then all creatures, even the non-human, bear the Word of God in a somewhat sacramental sense. As in the sacraments, God's Spirit seeks to speak through them. In Exodus 3 God speaks through a burning bush; in Numbers 22:28 Balaam's *donkey* is the mouth of God. And the Bible records a sacramental response of faith and praise *from* creation as it acknowledges the presence of its Creator. As Jesus rides into Jerusalem on Passion Sunday, he says (when the Pharisees are offended by the hosannas being offered Jesus by Jesus's disciples), "I tell you, if these were silent, the *stones* would shout out" (Luke 19:40, italics mine). Stones were, in fact, often set apart as witnesses, either to the covenant words spoken between God and the people (Josh. 24:27) or to cries of injustice to which the nations had become deaf (Hab. 2:11).

If donkeys and stones (let alone water, bread. and wine) can bear a word to, about, or from God, then surely our human neighbors who live in the community just outside our churches may be such a word for us, even when they don't call themselves believers. We would be wise to listen to them.

That's not always comfortable. I sometimes ask the seminary students I teach to invite community people who don't belong to a faith group to attend a barbecue and talk about their experiences of awe, wonder, mystery, God. Often at the end of the conversation participants from the community will say, "Thank you. This has been a wonderful experience. Usually the church wants to tell me something. This is the first time the church has listened to what I have to say."

It may help congregations listen to their communities if they remember that much of our cherished Bible has its origins outside Christian faith and Western culture. Hearing the Bible's strange word with humility can silence us Christians and teach us to listen to the outsider, to look for the presence of God clothed in the other. Such listening may not be comfortable. It leaves us vulnerable, because what God says through outsiders may challenge our understanding of the world. Our core values may be shaken. We may come to question the shorthand beliefs that allow us to function in society. Nonetheless, we need to hear it.

Of course, in all of this listening and speaking to, from, and about God, there is a wonderful circularity. Because God is clothed in creation, God-related words are spoken by creatures, but it is the Father, Son, and Spirit that impel their speaking. Paul hints at it when he says, "We do not know how to pray as we ought, but that very Spirit intercedes with sighs too deep for words" (Rom. 8:26). So as we listen to God and speak with God through each other, the Trinity knits us into the kind of community that Father, Son, and Spirit share among themselves.

It makes sense then that this book focuses on community-building tools that require conversation marked by deep listening. Appreciative inquiry and asset mapping are processes that encourage creative communication out of which new patterns of life and ministry can emerge.

Creative Conversation Is Adjustment to the Other

In science several streams of theoretical thought are examining the community-building power that comes from simple, effective communication that allows entities to *adjust* to each other, to take their neighbors into account. The physical sciences speak of it as *autopoiesis*, or self-organization. Autopoiesis refers to the way that patterns emerge in physical systems without an external agent imposing it. A simple example is crystallization, the appearance of a beautifully symmetric pattern of dense matter in a solution of randomly moving molecules. As the molecules encounter each other, they adjust, vibrating into positions that result in fewer collisions but closer, beautifully ordered connections to each other.

The biological and life sciences have developed similar theories. *Natural intelligence* examines the way in which the neural networks of living things organize themselves and grow. *Crowd psychology* looks at the way in which human groups organize without an external leader. (A good example is the Occupy movement that swept around the world in the fall of 2011. Though leaders emerged in each location, there appears to have been no single person or group directing the movement.) *Swarm theory* focuses on the group behavior of animals or insects such as ants and bees. In each case, the assumption is that organisms can solve problems and develop complex structures without any external direction, simply by communicating or taking each other into account.

National Geographic senior editor Peter Miller talks about swarm behavior in ants. He says:

> Ants aren't clever little engineers, architects, or warriors after all—at least not as individuals. When it comes to deciding what to do next, most ants don't have a clue. "If you watch an ant try to accomplish something, you'll be impressed by how inept it is," says Deborah M. Gordon, a biologist at Stanford University.
>
> How do we explain, then, the success of Earth's 12,000 or so known ant species? They must have learned something in 140 million years.
>
> "Ants aren't smart," Gordon says. "Ant colonies are." A colony can solve problems unthinkable for individual ants, such as finding the shortest path to the best food source, allocating workers to different tasks, or defending a territory from neighbors. As individuals, ants might be tiny dummies, but as colonies they respond quickly and effectively to their environment. . . .
>
> No one's in charge. No generals command ant warriors. No managers boss ant workers. The queen plays no role except to lay eggs. Even with half a million ants, a colony functions just fine with no management at all—at least none that we would recognize. It relies instead upon countless interactions between individual ants, each of which is following simple rules of thumb.[4]

Indian traffic seems to illustrate swarm theory. My first day in India, on the road to Agra, I was dismayed by the apparent chaos. Slow-moving bullocks, three-wheeled auto-rickshaws, elephants, trucks, cars, cows, camels, and motorcycles jostled for space with no heed to lanes or traffic rules. It would lead to deadly accidents and massive jams in North America. Yet traffic flows in India because people take each other into account. They communicate with honking horns or blinking lights ("I want to pass") or hand signals ("Go ahead" or "Wait"). It's not externally organized, but everyone gets to their destination.

We'll see in asset mapping that simple forms of communication between people about apparently unrelated resources can lead to marvelous, out-of-the-box ideas for strengthening communities. And both asset mapping and appreciative inquiry are about *listening* to people's stories, helping them articulate their own history and resources as the first step in love's communication.

I once heard a town councilor scolding churches for their approach to the homeless. She said, "What do the homeless really want? If you ask *them*, they say, 'Homes!' But what do you Christians always want to give them? Food, overnight shelter, clothing. That's nice, but the homeless don't want to have to move every night, go to the bathroom outside during the day, have no place to shower, spend winter days in the cold, eat strangers' food every meal. Why don't you *listen* to the people you want to help?"

Community Is a Web of Relationships

Earlier in this chapter I mentioned Einstein's general theory of relativity. As I said, he sees space-time not as an empty container into which people, planets, and galaxies have been placed but rather as composed of, and shaped by, the *relationships* between all that is. For Einstein the universe is *not* a stage and we the players on it. Rather the universe is a web of interconnecting, dynamically changing relationships into which we ourselves are woven.

In the same way, the Trinity shows us that the essence of community is in the bridged spaces *between* individuals. In fact, it is these relationships that *give* us our individual identities. Jesus is the Father's "only Son . . . who is close to the Father's heart" (John 1:14, 17). The Father is Jesus's "Abba" (Mark 14:36). The Spirit is the Spirit *of God* or the Spirit *of Jesus* and is sent by the Father and Son (John 15).

We can see a faint reflection of the identity-forming power of relationships in human development. A child's sense of self grows as parents call her by name, point out her body parts, tell her she's beautiful, hold her close, play with and feed her. We come to know ourselves as "Daddy's girl" or "John's son" or "Mommy's boy." If we are well treated and well regarded, we grow up well. If not, our selves form as stunted or broken. But in either case, because such relationships *create* our identities, they have remarkable power. Farmers who have been forced to leave their communities because of bankruptcy have told me that they feel as though they've "had a leg amputated." They couldn't imagine having an intact self apart from the relationships that sustained it.

Building healthy relationships, not starting new programs (as useful as those might be), is the most powerful result of using participatory community-building tools. The tools help congregations and communities develop a new self-image, see themselves as gifted and beloved, a people with a future. And they weave people's identities together so that commitment is increased and conflict does not easily pull them apart—which is a good thing, because the next two characteristics of healthy communities—difference and struggle—threaten to do just that.

Difference Is at the Heart of Community

There seems to be a default setting that operates in human relationships to *reduce* differences. Dating couples avoid controversial subjects (such as, "Should shopping really be your main source of entertainment?" or "I can't stand your mother!") and focus on their common interests. Churches debating volatile issues like abortion or same-sex marriage may split if they can't agree on a policy or theology, so they often drop the debate.

Communities frequently understand unity to be sameness or uniformity. That understanding generates a destructive push-pull effect. The push comes from the fact that unity understood as uniformity breeds fear of assimilation. If we must all be the same, we worry about having our own space overrun, our own patterns of life overwritten by others. So people push each other away and reinforce their boundaries, creating a zone of protection. This is most obvious perhaps in cities where crowded conditions encourage the building of high fences and anonymous isolation is expected. But it also occurs in rural settings. Small churches are often reluctant to merge because they are afraid of losing their own history and identity. Particularly if one of the merging partners is bigger than the other, they fear that they will be *sub*merged.

However, loneliness, the God-given gravity at the heart of community, makes complete separation a miserable experience for most. And in many contexts—rural communities or urban boardrooms, for example—it is obvious that we *can't* live without each other. If unity means uniformity, people may try to pull each other into conformity. They compete for social power, thinking, "If we must be together, and being together means uniformity, I'd at least prefer that everyone wears *my* uniform." Some give in to the pull, putting on the uniform of the powerful to avoid conflict. Those that don't conform or can't make others conform are pushed out, excluded, and depreciated in various ways.

Uniformity is the unity one finds in a brick or a sheet of white paper—unity as *sameness*. But there is another kind of unity—deep *integration*. That's what my puzzle-loving grandmother strove for as she fit thousands of unique jigsaw pieces into works of art.

The fact is that *difference*, not sameness, is at the base of creation. The universe exists because God apparently wanted something to *be* that was *not* God—something different, something other. Allowing creation the freedom to be different has certainly been humbling for God. From being all that was, God had to *contract* in a sense (to use the language of an old Jewish philosopher, Isaac Luria). God *made room* for creation. God invited difference into being.

We can see those differences at the deepest levels of reality. In the quantum world no single indivisible substance divides and recombines in different ways to make up everything else. Nor does there seem to be a single unified force of which the basic four (gravity, electromagnetism, and the weak and strong nuclear forces) are expressions—though physicists yearn to find one. From the smallest levels to the largest, diverse elements in close communication constitute creation. From string to quark to atom to molecule to cell to organism to planet to solar system to galaxy to universe(s), *integrated diversity* is the norm.

In this respect, creation reflects the God we've met in Christ. Hindus tell of *one* hidden God, Brahma, who is expressed in countless avatars (the 360-million-plus gods advertised in the New Delhi airport). But Christian experience begins with the

Three in One—the God of Israel, Jesus the Son, and the Spirit of Pentecost. Christians have no direct knowledge of a hidden divine substance commonly shared but individually expressed by these Three. Instead, what we see are the Three so deeply bound in loving relation that they can be described as indivisibly one.

God is whole, it seems, because all that truly belongs to God is found in the distinctions among the Three. God is Creator because the Father initiates, the Son shapes, the Spirit enervates. God is our Savior because the Spirit conceives the Son in Mary's womb, the Son suffers us in love, and the Father raises him, and in him all creation, to life.

Of course, trinitarian community is not just a simple division of labor—as if $^1/_3 + {}^1/_3 + {}^1/_3 = 1$. The ancient creeds confess that each divine person is *fully* God. But the Three are fully God only because the others "dwell within" each one, the same writers said. (The image of Russian nested dolls gives a vague sense of this indwelling.)

Divine diversity suggests that difference, in deep *loving* relationship, has enormous creative potential. The tools we will explore together further on in this book help to identify the many different gifts in a congregation and community and to connect them. They don't always feel natural to the participants, however. I notice that in asset-mapping exercises, for example, there is a strong tendency for participants to want to group *similar* gifts and resources. But it tends to paralyze the process. Only when participants begin to connect oddly divergent gifts do the really creative solutions emerge.

Struggle Is Normal and Necessary in Healthy Communities

Difference, even in a loving relationship, inevitably leads to struggle. When our son lived at home I would want the car to go to work; my son wanted it to pick up his girlfriend. Our differing needs generated some conflict. Sometimes it was settled by power ("I'm paying the insurance; I get first dibs"), sometimes by concession and compromise ("Okay, it's yours this time—mine the next"). Often my wife intervened ("Dear, why don't you let him drop you off at work before he picks up his girlfriend? A colleague can bring you home.").

In "The Social Doctrine of the Trinity: Some Problems," Anglican theologian Mark Chapman suggests that the ubiquitous presence of conflict in human relationships creates a problem if we try to imagine the Trinity as a model for community. He says that we tend to regard the relationships between the Three as simply harmonious—all willing the same thing, for example.[5] If this is the case, however, the Trinity is a far cry from anything we see in human (or any other natural) communities, because *struggle* has characterized the history of creation. Since God allows us the freedom to be *other* than God, creation's unfolding has taken many difficult and unfortunate turns. Galaxies have swallowed galaxies, meteors have wiped out life that has taken billions of years to develop.

However, God did not abandon us in creation. God did not leave us to be *other alone* but continues to sustain and support us (reflecting the *connected* difference that exists within the Trinity). Therefore those disasters haven't shut creation down. God opens up our future with new possibilities. For example, the Permian extinction, 245 million years ago, wiped out about 95 percent of the animals in the fossil record. But it opened up space for the dinosaurs to flourish for 180 million years. We mammals got our chance 65 million years ago when a huge meteor crashed into a shallow sea with a sulfur bed, kicking up a worldwide rain of sulfuric acid. We managed to survive, hiding in our small caves; the dinosaurs didn't. We have become human by facing enormous challenges to our existence and changing to meet and take advantage of them.

The Christian story is full of similar struggles. As Canadian theologian Douglas Hall points out in *God and Human Suffering*,[6] Adam and Eve wrestled with loneliness, limits, temptation, and anxiety in the Garden of Eden. Then Cain and Abel battled to gain divine favor. Israel struggled in Egypt and in the desert and in exile. The church has grappled with Gentile-Jew divisions, Roman persecution, and Protestant heretics. And Jesus of Nazareth—the highest expression of God's connection to creation—was tortured to death. Yet out of that tragedy came the resurrection and the promise that death could never have the last word in God's world.

Interestingly, the struggle the Bible narrates takes place not only between the characters in the Bible but also between its authors. For example, the early Christian church wrestled mightily with the meaning of Jesus's horrific death. Some imagined God as a God of retributive justice who took out the punishment for our sin on Jesus and who will ultimately take vengeance on Israel's enemies in Jesus's second coming. Others saw in Jesus's Father a God who ends human violence by absorbing it in divine love.

The biblical authors force *us* to struggle too. We cannot read the Bible without finding ourselves caught between polar opposites: one writer assures us that all will be saved (1 Cor. 15:22; Phil. 2:9; 1 Tim. 4:10; Rom. 5:18; and so on), another that some will be damned (John 3:18; Rev. 20:15; John 3:18; and so forth). We are warned that "you reap whatever you sow" (Gal. 6:7) and yet promised that "by grace you have been saved" (Eph. 2:4, 8) regardless of what we have done. We are assured that when the Messiah comes the nations will "beat their swords into plowshares" (Isa. 2:4), yet Jesus says, "Do not think that I have come to bring peace to the earth; I have not come to bring peace, but a sword" (Matt. 10:34). We are told that climate events are not related to human behavior: "He makes his sun rise on the evil and on the good, and sends rain on the righteous and on the unrighteous" (Matt. 5:45). Yet Israel escapes Egypt on the basis of plagues selectively applied by God (Exod. 9:25, 26) and Israel suffers a three-and-a-half-year drought for its sins (1 Kings 17; James 5:17).

You see what I mean. The Bible throws us into the ring to wrestle with law and gospel, hope and lament, fear and love, retribution and forgiveness. But it also directs us to throw ourselves on the mercy of God, who sustains us as we seek our way through these difficult dynamics in human life.

Given that struggle is endemic to all created, human, and even Christian life, can we also imagine that such struggle belongs to the life of the *divine* community? The Bible suggests that it does. Father, Spirit, and Son wrestle order from chaos in Genesis 1. Their labor is ongoing, because chaos is never overcome in this creation. In the book of Revelation, the sea—the symbol of chaos—is permanently resident in front of God's throne. Chaos is not eliminated until this old creation is finally transformed at the end of history.

Another example: a "tempter" or "adversary" is allowed to inhabit not only the Garden of Eden but, according to the book of Job, also has a place in the divine court. In Mark 1, the Spirit *drives* Jesus into the wilderness to be "tested" by this adversary (which is what the name *Satan* means). As the word *drive* (or "casts out") suggests, the struggle was not only within Jesus but also between Jesus and the Spirit, who does the driving, and the Father, who wills it. However, the struggle is a productive one: Jesus's trust in the Father is deepened as he is forced to choose between relying on the Father's baptismal promise, "You are my beloved Son," and proving to Satan that he is indeed that Son. His resolve is strengthened as he considers and rejects Satan's offer of a shortcut to gaining followers that would bypass the cross.

Jesus struggles again with the Father in the Garden of Gethsemane. The rock opera *Jesus Christ Superstar* highlights the conflictual elements when Jesus prays, "Show me there's a reason for you wanting me to die. You're far too keen on where and how, but not so hot on why!" Certainly Jesus's cry from the cross, "My God, my God, why have you forsaken me?" exposes a divine relationship that can include even feelings of betrayal—definitely more than simple, untroubled harmony.

It seems that just as an athlete with Olympic ambitions must struggle with muscle pain, with her own desires for rest and food, and with multiple assaults on self-esteem, so too Jesus grew through struggle. When Father, Son, and Spirit drew into their life the history of humanity, they opened themselves to conflict that would challenge their love for each other and for us at its deepest level. Yet that struggle is a fruitful one that will ultimately lead to the reconciliation of all creation in God.

So healthy community development does not proceed by denying difference. Conflict will occur. But fruitful development takes place in a context of love. Differences are explored with respect. Using tools such as appreciative inquiry and asset mapping allows the challenge implicit in difference to be moved out of a very personal space, where participants might be threatened by the other, into an objective exercise that allows each to listen for understanding. Only after deep listening (though not necessarily full agreement) is it possible to make common plans for ministry.

Power Multiplies When It Is Distributed

Of course, not all conflict is fruitful. It can be highly destructive. This is particularly true when individuals or institutions act like a vacuum, collecting resources or people, concentrating power. One sees a tendency to concentrate power throughout our society. Farms get bigger, school districts amalgamate, corporations take over other corporations. Wealth is concentrated in fewer hands. This is the pyramid model, which draws power and resources up to the top. It happens in churches too when pastors make themselves indispensable, focusing ministry on their own skills. They grow in the eyes of the people, but all others diminish as power is concentrated in the pastor's hands.

That concentration of power is exactly the opposite of what we see in the Trinity. The Son gives up divine privilege, empties himself to take on human form. The Spirit gives the Son life in Mary's womb. (What a loss of control that is—to put the incarnate God helpless into the hands of a young peasant!) At Jesus's baptism in the Jordan, the Father and Spirit draw attention to the Son and honor him. The Father trusts the Son with the mission of reconciling humanity. "All things have been handed over to me by my Father," Jesus says in Matthew 11. The Spirit empowers Jesus for that mission. "The Spirit of the Lord is upon me," Jesus says in Luke 4:18, "because he has anointed me to bring good news to the poor."

Yet Jesus doesn't draw all the power and attention to himself. When Lazarus is raised in John 11, Jesus attributes the resuscitation to the glory of God, giving the Father credit and not claiming it for himself. Facing the horror of the cross in the Garden of Gethsemane the Son gives up control—"Your will be done"—and then as he is dying, he relinquishes all power, sighing, "Into your hands I commend my spirit."

Out of death, the Father raises the Son in the power of the Spirit. At Pentecost Father and Son release control of God's mission in the world to the Holy Spirit. Though he is leaving, Jesus reassures the disciples in John 14:16, 25: "I will ask the Father, and he will give you another Advocate, to be with you forever. . . . The Holy Spirit, whom the Father will send in my name, will teach you everything." He breathes the Spirit on them.

The Bible tells us that when the trumpet sounds, Jesus will return in glory and there will be one more exchange of power. "Then comes the end," Paul says in 1 Corinthians 15:24, 28, when Christ "hands over the kingdom to God the Father so that God [the Trinity] may be all-in-all."

Because power in God is distributed instead of concentrated, the ministry of the Father, Son, and Spirit is multiplied. Because power is handed over, the gifts of each are able to blossom fully. Their differences become fruitful. In the mutual interaction of their gifts, the Three are wholly One, wholly God, for us.

That's the kind of relationship that the Three in One draws us into. Right from the beginning, they share power with us and invite us to share power with each other. The Creator gives to our planet the power to "bring forth" a variety of creatures (Gen. 1:13, 20, 24). God breathes the Spirit into our red clay, empowering us to live. We are told to be "fruitful and multiply"—and are given the power of creative reproduction (making new and unique beings, not simply copies of the original). We're given powerful brains and opposable thumbs so that we can learn how to play the tuba, plant gardens, build computers.

Of course, sharing power is a risky thing. I can't say that we have used power particularly well. But it's a risk the Three in One keeps taking because they love us—and because it's the only way they can develop among us the communal life they share.

Jesus's servant ministry was certainly power*ful*. But it was not one in which he exercised power *over* others (making them do what he wanted). Nor did he exercise power *for* others (doing for them what they could do for themselves). He didn't provide power *under* others (serving as a safety net for them when they couldn't function). These forms of power, when used consistently, infantilize communities. They make them dependent and keep communities from developing their full capacities.

Instead Jesus exercised power *into* others. He tested and trained his disciples. He forced them to sweat and struggle and stretch their understanding of justice and the kingdom of God. Then with the Father, he sent the Spirit to dwell in them: "You will receive power when the Holy Spirit has come upon you; and you will be my witnesses in Jerusalem, in all Judea and Samaria, and to the ends of the earth," Jesus says in Acts 1:8. The giving of the gospel mission into human hands is perhaps God's greatest act of empowerment in our experience.

Of course, giving such an enormous responsibility to that first, tiny band of disciples might seem like a foolish way to get a message out. If I want my students to know that a class is cancelled, I don't tell one of them and ask them to pass it on. I send an e-mail to each person individually. So why didn't the Three in One just communicate the gospel directly to all of us at the same time? Perhaps because although such an arrangement would establish a relationship between each of us and God, it wouldn't help us to relate to each other. God wants to *build community*, to connect us with each other. So the Spirit and the Son gave the story to twelve, who gave it to others, who gave it to others, who gave it to us. As we share our stories with each other, those stories empower us. Links of trust are forged, our lives are interwoven. Community forms.

The community-building tools described in this book give power away. In both of them, community and ministry plans are developed from the bottom up. *Appreciative inquiry* assumes that wisdom for ministry resides in the people. They are not told how to do ministry but are interviewed as to their experience of what works. *Asset mapping* helps people discover the unexpected resources in their lives and connect them in creative ways with others'.

THE LEADER'S ROLE

In using these tools, it is not the leader's job to cast a vision or imagine a future for the congregation or the community. Ideas emerge as people listen to each other and talk to each other. The leader's task is to facilitate, coalesce, and connect ideas, to catalyze and stimulate the development of vision.

The community-building power of these tools does not come from top-down, externally imposed designs of a human or divine engineer. Rather the power resides in the people, inspired by the Spirit. The loving interaction of human differences, creatively connected, leads to wonderful new structures of life and ministry.

CHAPTER 2

Public Church

A Mixed Blessing?

If God's mission in the world is to build communities that reflect something of the Trinity, one might assume that churches would want to get on board. And many have. But the history of churches' engagement with their communities is a checkered one. In part that's because the religious ideas they transmit have great power for both good and ill. Beliefs are powerful; they shape our social and economic behavior. Christian belief is anchored in a transformative story that can challenge destructive worldviews embedded in our society. But that story itself can be destructive when it is not communicated clearly and contextually. I suspect this is also true of faith traditions other than Christianity. Let me share a few stories.

RELIGION: BUILDING COMMUNITY, TEARING IT DOWN

One of the Bengali villages I visited in rural India had experienced a great deal of distress due to the high number of children suffering from dysentery. Many babies died from it. Other children were left with serious disabilities. In the year before my arrival, an NGO had begun working with the mothers in that village. The women formed a self-help group that focused on sanitation, food safety, and access to potable water. As a result of their efforts, the childhood death rate dropped to a fraction of what it had been.

I was curious about the role local religious leaders might have had in these dramatic changes and asked one of the women about it. She replied, "When we asked the priest why our children were dying, he told us it was the gods' punishment because we didn't come to worship. But now we know it was just bad hygiene. I think they wanted us to come and worship so that they will get more money for their livelihood."

A second experience took place in the foothills of the Himalayas. A farmer had invited me to join him, his family, and two friends to greet the day. We sat together in a small, open-walled hut overlooking the source waters of the Ganges. As the first rays of sunshine struck the floor of the hut, the farmer lighted a bowl filled with chips of dried cow dung. Smoke curled up while he hummed a mantra in Hindu tradition. Then as the fire died, he gathered the ashes and took them outside to be scattered on the fields. Afterward he showed us around the farm. He said that he was no longer using chemical fertilizers—just a rich compost he created from cow manure and roadside weeds. He controlled pests with manure poultices and various natural means, avoiding herbicides and pesticides. Land that had been damaged by heavy use of chemicals was gradually regaining its fertility.

I asked him how he had come to this new way of farming. He said, "A yogi gave me a copy of the Vedas [Hindu scriptures]. I read that the land is the body of God. The yogi taught me that I must treat the land with more respect, not polluting it or robbing it of its vitality. The Vedas showed me the way."

This farmer found in his religion a resource for farming that is both sustainable and profitable. The productivity of his land is gradually increasing, and his certified organic produce gets much better prices.

Stories from Canada and the United States

The ambivalent role religion plays in the life of these rural Hindus mirrors what I have witnessed in Canada and the United States. I spent several years researching the influence of the Christian church on people who were going through farm bankruptcy. Many times I heard Christian farmers speak of having been "abandoned by God" when they lost their farms. One woman sitting beside me on a plane told of watching her parents attempt suicide when their farm failed. She cried, "What did we do to deserve this?" I also heard others whose operations were in the black say modestly when I asked about their success, "We've been blessed by God."

Both the solvent and the insolvent had picked up the belief that there is a direct connection between their financial situation and God's attitude toward them. A profitable operation was regarded as a blessing from God (with the hidden implication that it was a reward for good behavior or good management). Insolvency was treated as a sign that God has withdrawn the blessing, that one was cursed (probably because of misbehavior).

This sort of religious influence is oppressive in a community. It locks those who are suffering into a prison of silent shame. "The wolf's at the door, the walls are closing in, and *I couldn't talk to anyone*" is how one farmer described it. Paralyzed by fear of the community's disapproval, many rural people I interviewed who were in financial trouble were unable to ask for the emotional and practical help they needed. Somehow their faith community had failed to communicate the good news that our worth and value as people is given and safeguarded by God's love for us.

Without that assurance, shame kept those farmers from reaching out for help. It also kept them from sharing equipment with their neighbors or farming cooperatively in other ways, even when it was more profitable to do so. They were afraid of opening their books to neighbors, lest the neighbors spot a weakness and lose respect for them. Some told me that in order to mask their financial problems the husband bought a new pickup truck or the wife bought expensive clothing. They were willing to make their financial situation worse in order to keep up appearances—because they felt that their personal worth was set by their neighbors, not by God.

While this shame-based thinking is common in popular religion, it flies in the face of the central Christian witness. Jesus, the Righteous One, was at various points homeless, unemployed, and ultimately executed in the most humiliating fashion for several capital crimes. Yet God raised him from the dead. In Jewish understanding, only the *righteous* are raised. Jesus's resurrection clearly indicates that divine approval is not dependent on one's social, legal, or financial status.

Shame-based thinking also depends on an individualistic doctrine of providence, failing to see that the biblical promises are given to *communities as a whole*. For example the promise in Proverbs 13:21—that righteousness will lead to prosperity—makes sense when applied to a whole nation: when all members relate rightly to each other, all experience well-being. But it is nonsense when applied to individuals, because innocent individuals may be victims of injustice at the hands of others. Or they may suffer the freedom that exists within creation for conditions to occur (such as weather) that benefit some and not others.

So I told that woman on the plane, "God loves you and is proud of you, just the way you love your own daughter and are proud of her. Your worth doesn't depend on how well you manage the farm or how well markets and weather cooperate. You can't lose your worth or do anything to increase it. It's yours. It's a gift given and guaranteed by God." She began to cry and said, "I used to go to church—but I never heard that." I suspect she may have heard it in general terms. But it had never been brought out onto her farm. To be good news for her, the gospel had to be given the clothing of her context. Certainly the body of Christ has a gracious, renewing story to tell; but it is useless unless Christian congregations take that story out of the church and connect it to the specific realities of our world.

Church Engaged with Community
but Living Beyond It

It may be that the church moves from being a positive element in its community to one that is destructive when it fails to maintain a critical tension. If, as we have maintained, the Trinity is our model for church and community, then on the one hand the church is called to be holy—that is, to be *unlike* its surrounding community in some ways. Unlike our world, the church should value human life and communities not because of their economic productivity, conformity to social norms, or population size but on the basis of the gracious unconditional hospitality extended between Father, Son, and Spirit.

On the other hand, the Trinity is not a sealed, self-contained unit enjoying their love for each other in splendid isolation. Their outgoing love keeps the church's view turned outward, reminding it not to become a self-congratulating, navel-gazing sect. The church has been given an alternative worldview *for the sake of the world*. It is called to be apostolic.

BARRIERS TO CHURCH-COMMUNITY ENGAGEMENT

Many churches in North America, however, don't engage their communities deeply. There are various reasons, some generated by the church, others by the societies around it. Here are a few that may need to be examined and deconstructed for some in your congregation before it can move into mission with full commitment.

Public Suppression of Faith Talk

In Canada, public religious talk is often treated as embarrassing self-disclosure—like airing the details of one's personal finances or intimate sexual life with strangers. Faith is regarded as a slightly shameful private preference. In some provinces public faith talk is banned within certain occupations, such as government and primary public education.

So it is not surprising that Canadian churches tend to keep their religious practices hidden behind stained glass windows. They function, if the metaphor can be forgiven, somewhat like a private swingers' club. The club is glad to receive newcomers, but the members aren't keen to advertise their membership publicly.

In the United States, the situation is somewhat similar. Sociologist Peter Berger has joked that if India is the most religious country in the world and Sweden the least, then America is a country of Indians governed by Swedes.[1] According to Jeffrey Stout, Princeton professor of religion, American public suppression of religious conversation springs from a widely held view that there are only two options for democracy: a secularism that excludes public religious conversation or a fundamentalism that forces it. Secularism, he says, has tended to carry the day in public circles.[2]

Nonetheless, American efforts to combine explicit religious positions with political platforms have had more success in the past few decades than similar efforts in Canada. In fact, under the Bush administration a good deal of funding was moved from public coffers to support faith-based community-building efforts. Some churches welcomed the move. However, others have deplored it. They see it not as forging partnerships between churches and social institutions but as a downloading of responsibility for social programs onto a small segment of the population. Churches want to *add* their gifts to the general community-building enterprise, not necessarily become replacement administrators of it.

My own sense of the reticence (at least among Canadians) to talk *publicly* about people's deep worldviews—our visions of what is good community—is that such talk is regarded as destabilizing. It has the potential for conflict. Not having the courage to struggle for a deeply integrated diversity (God's kind of unity), we replace talk about what is *good* with pragmatic, less divisive talk about *rights* and *policies.* Rights are about our *freedom* to pursue the good; policies have to do with the *ways* by which we pursue the good. But both mean little unless we have first discussed exactly *what that good is* or looks like. And to a large extent, Canadians, at least, aren't talking about that. Pragmatic conversation seems less potentially fractious.

So in the end, public conversation bogs down in arguments about *how* we will operate as societies without really knowing *what* we are trying to achieve or *why.* We talk about means without knowing the ends. My suspicion is that the real ends to which our nations are being driven are the (publicly unexamined) visions of the good held by those with power.

Separation of the Spheres of Life

When I talk about God's community-building mission, I often get feedback suggesting that while such community-building is fine, the church must be careful not to get involved in politics or economics or social work. That's "secular stuff," not the spiritual work that the church has been given, audience members assert.

This response, it seems to me, depends on a basic thinking-mistake in our theology and our sociology. In our thought processes, we separate out aspects of life so that we can analyze and categorize. But we can then come to assume that life itself actually has such divisions. In fact, life is like a tapestry on a weaver's loom. We may follow a thread or pattern element with our eyes, but the threads themselves are bound into the fabric, deeply connected to each other, and cannot be actually separated without destroying the cloth.

Theologically, for Protestants the thinking mistake often stems from Luther's misnamed "two kingdom ethic," from which popular and constitutional language about the "separation of church and state" has developed.[3] It must first be said that for Luther, God reigns in all creation—not just the church. He cannot imagine any arena in creation that is outside God's influence; there is no "secular" realm, in the modern sense of the word, for Luther.

What Luther does do, drawing on Paul's letter to the Romans, is identify two *aspects* of life: He notes that God has a unique way of *governing* each of those aspects of life: God speaks good news (gospel) to bring hope, forgiveness, and new life to the spirit, and God speaks law to bring good order, stability, and health to the flesh.[4] We in turn apprehend and respond to the gospel through faith (deep trust in God); we apprehend the law through reason and respond to it through works. Certainly Luther does see the church's special gift to the world to be the gospel. But he was also very concerned about the *ordering* of human life according to the dynamics revealed in the life of Jesus as he relates to the Father and the Spirit. So for him Christian mission is not just about saving souls but also about bringing hope and order to people in the concrete realities of their personal and community lives.

Luther, in his writings, does muddy the waters at times by using *kingdom of God* and *kingdom of the world*—or of the devil—language. But when he does so his intention is not to distinguish two separate regions of human life. Rather his goal is to distinguish God's effort to bring law and gospel to all aspects of human life from those habits and attitudes in the world (inspired by Satan,

Luther would say) that bring death, guilt, and chaos. Liberation theologians might call these "worldly" norms and practices *hegemonies*. They are worldviews promoted by the powerful to justify oppression and domination, sometimes using religious language, sometimes couched in atheistic or pseudoscientific terms.

Precisely in order to counter these destructive influences, Luther refuses to allow the church to keep its hands off worldly matters. Instead, he sees it as the church's responsibility to speak to the world, and to build in the world God's vision for healthy humanity. So he says:

> Now if a preacher in his official capacity says to kings and princes and to all the world "Thank and fear God and keep His commandments" he is not meddling in the affairs of secular government. On the contrary he is thereby serving and being obedient to the highest government. . . . For He is one God, the same Lord of all, of the one as well as of the other. Therefore they [the church and the state] should all be identical in their obedience and should even be mixed into one another like one cake, every one of them helping the other to be obedient. . . .[5]

Luther's words help us recapture a vision of God outside the sanctuary.

Sociologically, we make a similar thinking mistake when we view communities as being divided into supposedly independent *sectors* (like the departments or agencies in a state or provincial government). The mistake is compounded when we assume that one of these is most important (the spiritual or economic or political) and that if we attend to that one, the others will all come in line in a trickle-down fashion. Churches might think, "If we just get folks saved, their lives, their finances, will get straightened out." Business folks think, "If we can only get that lumber company to build their mill here, the jobs and cash inflow will make this town a happy place."

Community developers around the world, however, have found that this isn't so. While sectors can be a useful conceptual framework for analytic purposes, no corresponding set of separate entities exists in real communities. All aspects of a community are interconnected and interactive. Addressing just one aspect in isolation from the others distorts community life and usually brings unintended consequences. Perhaps an oil crew descends on a small town. The business in the restaurants and hotels picks up, but sex workers and drug dealers start showing up to meet the crew's demands. Bars get noisier and more violent. The health care facilities are overtaxed. The spirit of the town changes.

Or an example from another side: cultural and spiritual assumptions (such as the notion that weed-free fields and new machinery are a sign of prosperity and God's favor) can inhibit adopting valuable technologies such as organic farming, which doesn't use herbicides and is less machinery and energy intensive.[6] One farmer told me, "I've done the calculations—I know I'd be better off financially if I went organic, but I can't stand the fact that there would be more weeds in my field, and people would drive by and say, 'Oh, that poor Johnson boy. His dad used to keep those fields so clean'"!

As we think about the church's contribution to God's community-building mission then, we need to consider not only what the church properly has to offer but also how its gifts might connect, interact, and overlap with the elements of community life that we don't normally regard as spiritual.

The Shame of Suffering

In part because of these sacred-secular separations, congregations tend to focus on individual care, often in private, behind professional screens of confidentiality. Unfortunately, the impact of those individual hurts on the wider community is often neglected. I have watched several denominations deal with clergy who committed sexual offenses. In most cases the focus was on either the offender or the victims. But the congregations and surrounding communities experienced enormous grief and shame that wasn't always well cared for. People who have come to identify deeply with a place or a group *will* share the shame and the grief of its members. They can't help doing so. Their experience reflects Paul's in 1 Corinthians 12:26 that "if one member suffers, all suffer together." And it reflects the ancient conviction that the suffering of Christ was shared by Father and Spirit in a brokenhearted love that would not wall itself away from him.[7]

One might think that shared suffering would generate empathy in the community for individual sufferers, and sometimes it does. But more often it feels to the community as though the individual sufferer has in some way wounded the *community,* exposed it to a deadly virus or to public ridicule (especially if media get involved). And so people avoid that member to escape further contagion. Or they engage in coffee-room critique that again distances them from the member's distress or behavior.

When shared shame leads to broken relationships, who will care for such communities if not the church? Who else knows how to mount a public ritual that allows for the airing of issues, general lament, prayers for those hurt and the community as a whole, and reconciliation and blessing? Who else can remind them that God chooses to be in broken places and holds this community—its past, its present, its broken members, and its public reputation— in the hands of Divine Love?

Thankfully, many churches do just that. In a rural town, I saw two clergy mobilize their congregations to prevent banks from taking a community member's land after the banks had foreclosed on the property (called "farm gate defenses"). Another accompanied his parishioner to debt review meetings to ensure that the parishioner was treated fairly and with respect. One of my students developed a liturgy for leaving a farm. In it, the family and some neighbors and church friends walked from house to barn to field celebrating God's gifts in each place, praying and reading Scripture, grieving together, and looking hopefully toward the future.

One of my urban parishioners worked with me to create a service for people who are unemployed. We tried to communicate clearly, in worship and in public practice, "Your job does not define you. You are a good person, beloved of God, respected by us. No matter what happens to you financially and personally, we will stand with you. We care about you and your family. We need you in our community."

In each case these leaders brought their confidence in God's unconditional grace into public life. They treated people in difficulty not with pity but with honor, looking them in the eye, acknowledging that they are people of worth and capability.

Churches' Palliative Care Mindset

A final barrier to church-community engagement is the weariness and depression that sets in for some churches that have experienced a steady succession of losses over the years. Congregations that once bemoaned the excessive noise of children in worship mourn that they now echo with the voices of only an elderly remnant. Often their eyes fix on the halcyon days of the 1950s and '60s, when boomer youth filled the pews. They long to be young again but feel old, impoverished, dying.

A vicious circle is at work here, of course. Churches that become isolated from their communities, and their mission in the process, tend to lose their members. Few want to stay in, and even fewer want to join, an enterprise that is rudderless, self-focused, and preoccupied with the fear of death.

Church judicatories spend much time and money devising ways to *revitalize* these congregations. But in a sense, bringing them back to life isn't the point; giving them a *reason to live* is. Erwin McManus, pastor of an innovative, international congregation in Los Angeles, notes in his book *An Unstoppable Force: Daring to Become the Church God Had in Mind* that there is no promise in the Bible that ensures the survival of churches. Their purpose is to witness to and serve their communities. *Witness*, he points out, is the same word as *martyr* in New Testament Greek: "Christian families, tribes and communities have been persecuted and brutally killed for their faith. They didn't survive. Yet they left a witness. The purpose of the church cannot be to survive or even to thrive but to serve. And sometimes servants die in the process."[8]

Perhaps then, the task of Christian leadership is to lead churches out of palliative care back into the world. Strong enough or not, congregations are called to serve as long as God gives them life.

Exercised in the power of God's Spirit, that service will be a public challenge to the forces that dismantle community life.

The Gospel for Communities

It is worth saying again: *God's love for the world is directed as much toward communities* as toward human individuals. We saw in chapter 1 that God's love for Israel saturates the biblical story. Yahweh's love letter to Zion in Isaiah 62 speaks of her as God's beloved bride, God's delight, an image repeated in the New Testament as well (Eph. 5:25; Rev. 21:9ff). That language is more than metaphor. Zion is not simply a collection of individuals that resembles a human bride. She is presented as a self-conscious being who lives in dynamic, committed relationship with God. Paul goes even further to speak of the church as the beloved "body" of Christ (1 Cor. 12; Eph. 5:23). He addresses his letters primarily to communal expressions of this body (at Ephesus, Corinth, etc.) much like the letters to the seven churches in Revelation.

We may be reluctant to give personality and consciousness to communities. Yet we've seen that our own body is itself a community of trillions and still has a persistent sense of identity and self-awareness. Towns and cities have it too. Though (as in our own bodies) there is growth and death and change within them, they tend to have distinctive personalities that persist over time. Toronto has a culture and history much different from Los Angeles or Bawlf, Alberta. Even towns a few miles apart are unique. Though they are constantly in some flux, each is recognizably home to those who live there.

So it is not unreasonable to imagine, particularly in view of the consistent biblical witness, that God *loves* communities. God places a high *value* on them that is unassailable and is not determined by their size or economic power. And God's promises (and warnings) to communities constitute a saving *word*—gospel and law—that begs for a messenger to convey it to them. The church, itself a community that is the recipient of that saving word, is God's messenger to the wider world communities.

This word, at its heart, is a word of *grace,* a wonderful gift of *hope.* Churches act and speak from the confidence that, embraced by a gracious and omnipotent God, the future of the communities they serve is truly open. The past and present can't hold them down. God's love for them—not market or demographic trends—is in charge. As God said to Israel's remnant community through the prophet Jeremiah: "I know the plans I have for you, . . . plans for your welfare and not for harm, to give you a future with hope" (Jer. 29:11).

THE GIFTS CHURCHES BRING TO THEIR COMMUNITIES

Trusting then that Christian churches truly do have something essential to offer to community well-being, here are a few thoughts (not exhaustive) about what they might contribute.

Head Space

Communities often succumb to trend worship or inevitability thinking. It's the thought form futurists depend on to pay the bills. The assumption is, "Things are going in a certain direction and will likely keep going that way." One might call it fatalism or a perceived law of social momentum. So when house prices are rising, people speculate on real estate, assuming prices will just keep going up, which of course pushes prices higher. When rural communities lose members, they fall into the vicious circle of assuming that nothing they can do will reverse the trend, so why try. And when they don't try, the loss continues, reinforcing their conviction that there is nothing they can do. Inevitability, this thinking locks communities into small planning boxes.

But of course history doesn't travel in straight lines. Community life oscillates, twists and turns, folds back on itself, and is interrupted by critical surprises. In *Christianity and Science,* Roman Catholic theologian John Haught suggests that novelty can be said to characterize all creation.[9] Who could have predicted by examining a bit of dense plasma in the moments after the big bang that one day a universe would develop with elements that are self-conscious, can sing opera, and read and write this book? Haught says we tend to think of time as being pushed forward—as if the past determines the future, as if the future is no more than the sum effect of all prior causes. But what if time is like a stream and we are standing in it, facing the future? The future is flowing to meet us, turning into the present and then into the past. If that is so—and the constant newness of life suggests it may be—then the future is truly open. We can't see what is around the bend coming toward us, but the possibilities are endless.

The church can give its towns and cities head space, room to hope. An open future unlocks imaginations imprisoned by despair or fatalism so they can respond creatively to life's stresses. The church tells the story of a God who saw his Son fall into a nightmare of betrayal, capital charges, and death and yet (great surprise!) raised that Son to indestructible life. The church claims that ancient hates and corrupt states, even the powers of death and hell, have no ultimate authority in Jesus's life—or our community's—because it is held by One who raises the dead. Such a God is our future and comes to meet us every moment.

Faith stories have the power to reframe reality, for good or ill. The wars being waged now in the Middle East, in Iraq and Afghanistan, are essentially wars of revenge. They are fuelled by stories of historic assaults on the honor of nations (and therefore the honor of their gods), assuming that honor can be restored only by retributive violence. Such narratives are deeply destructive because they focus on blame and punishment. They assume that hurting the one who hurts you somehow makes everything all right.

But religious stories have great power for hope and reconciliation as well. Stories that focus on identifying *God's* saving activity in dark circumstances (rather than what sin or Satan is doing to destroy us) can help communities move past blame and shame to healthy change. They arouse the energy needed to move on from the pain of the past.

I remember the effect that telling the stories of God's activity had on the theological consortium out of which I work. Our

dream of constructing a common building and integrated program had been crushed by a sudden loss of government and university funding. A couple of the schools involved came to the edge
of closure. Tensions began to develop as personnel were forced to
leave, and some communal depression set in.

One day members of the Joint Anglican-Lutheran Commission
visited our campuses and asked if they could meet with our facul-
ties in a common session. They wanted to find out what was working in our ecumenical partnership. As we went around the circle
and shared stories of successful cooperation, a growing sense of
relief and excitement became palpable in the room. Much more
was happening together than we were aware of. We'd been measuring our relationship by the failure of a dream, not by the reality
of what we had between us. The stories became part of a larger
narrative of hospitality that led to one of the schools moving in
with the one where I teach, helping to stabilize both.

In difficult situations, appreciative inquiry can function as a
"theology of the cross," as the Canadian theologian Douglas John
Hall uses the term. That is, appreciative inquiry discerns in the
darkness of our present crucifixion the moving of God's hand. It
gives congregations and communities the courage to reach out
and grasp that hand in hope of new life.

A survey of seventy-eight comprehensive, community-based
initiatives across Canada by the Pan-Canadian Community Development Learning Network concluded in its report, "Successful strategies to address poverty and exclusion require sustained
investments that target not just income and employment but . . .
attitudes and aspirations."[10] Little can change in a community if it
is locked into a mindset that can imagine the future only as the
status quo or a black hole. But churches have a narrative that can
reawaken and reeducate community hopes.

In fact, once a community begins to hope, to believe it is capable
of being well, it is already better. We tend to measure well-being
by what people *have* or *do*. But deep down we know that what
they are *capable* of is what matters most. The classic comparison
is a fasting monk and a starving child. Both have the same caloric
intake and nutritional deficiency, but we regard their well-being

much differently. The monk, unlike the child, has the *capability* to be adequately nourished.

A community that believes God is on its side, a community that has chronicled the history of God's work in its midst (appreciative inquiry), a community that has taken stock of its resources (asset mapping) is a community that knows it is capable of choosing a future different from its present, no matter what the trend. That confidence brings a tremendous freedom.

The Bible's story challenges us to dream of not just any future, however, but one that is different in many respects from the future set out by the reigning "isms" of our age. (I call them savage capitalism, technological determinism, and social Darwinism). The Bible suggests that it is not just the economically and technically fittest who will survive. Indeed, if that were the case, in the end only one would be left, unable to reproduce! The extinction philosophies that drive our world are challenged by the biblical worldview in which the weak are regarded as essential to the well-being of communities, in which "the members of the body that seem to be weaker are indispensable" and "if one member suffers, all suffer together with it" (1 Cor. 12:22, 26).

The Bible stimulates the exercise of a *rebellious imagination*. It enables us to conceive of, and work toward, other worlds.

Truth Telling

Jesus's constant iteration "the kingdom of heaven is like . . ." is his way of creating awareness that community life can be lived differently from the way the present arrangements allow. He tells an alternate truth in his parables.[11] But Jesus also speaks to ungodly powers in a very direct fashion. Ched Myers, in his eye-opening commentary on Mark, explores the political implications of some of these challenges.[12] Myers describes how Jesus calls into question Caesar's "divine right" of taxation when Jesus says, "Give to the emperor the things that are the emperor's, and to God the things that are God's" (Mark 12:17). He challenged political power, because every Jew knew that *all things* are God's and that Jesus was teaching that Caesar therefore had "rights" only derivatively, that is, according to God's will. When Jesus drives a herd of pigs over a cliff, he challenges the Roman destruction of Gerasa and the empire's replacement of Judean agriculture with corporate hog farming for export (5:1–15). He publicly calls the temple administrators "robbers" for their efforts to fleece women, the poor, and foreigners particularly, preventing them from going to worship unless they bought sacrifices at exorbitant prices and exchange rates (11:17). Examples could be drawn from other Gospels too: Jesus interferes in Judean justice when he speaks up for the woman caught in adultery, reminding the stoners that they themselves have sinned (John 8:3–11).

Churches around the world play a critical role in truth telling, advocacy, and political action with those whose rights are being trampled. Although this work is more obvious in Africa and Latin America, one can point to many examples from our own context. People like Martin Luther King Jr. or Tommy Douglas are historic paradigms of church leaders working against systemic oppression. In my own neighborhood, I recently witnessed a deeply moving celebration culminating a decade of cooperation between Mennonites, Lutherans, and the Stony Knoll First Nation to recover their stolen treaty rights.

Talking Space

Transformative public conversation, of course, requires a space for talking. Communities host spaces such as coffee shops where people bitch and brag about life's happenings or where occasional public forums are held. But for the talk to have the focus and intensity needed to spark real change, a more intentional conversation structure is needed. This is particularly true in urban centers. There individuals don't consistently see each other outside work. They meet one group of people occasionally for racquetball, another every second or third Sunday at church, and a third group at the community theater. So it's hard to carry on a consistent conversation in depth over time.

The problem is compounded by the impression that individual voices no longer have much weight in the public arena. As global fences have come down, enormous concentrations of power have formed in politics, economics, and entertainment. When ordinary people enter traditional public space, they are often facing behemoth conversation partners. It is easy for them to feel that anything they might say would have as much effect as a whisper in a hurricane. So they vote less, write fewer letters to companies and legislators, and are less likely to participate in town hall meetings.

The Internet, of course, has become a popular substitute for civic engagement. But its community-changing power generally lies in linking people to organizations that have buildings, funds, and leaders.

The church is one of those organizations. It is a wonderful but generally underrecognized space for ordinary folks to exchange ideas about values and social policies. (By *space* I mean both the physical space of a church and the social space of an intentional gathering. The community may not always be willing to enter the building but may be open to join an arranged conversation.) Church space gives community members a chance to practice the skills of listening and persuasion that are necessary for life in public. It is a space size that fits between the intimate privacy of family talk and the vast fishbowl of national news media or political debate. It's a space where people can test out their public voice with reasonable risk. They gain the confidence and build the partnerships that make it possible to take action for change locally, and even globally.

These skills are developed even (especially!) when people take different sides in the conversation. When I first began writing this chapter, service workers at our university are on strike. Since the university is the largest employer in town, most churches have members who are either in the union or in management. Some churches took the opportunity to help train their people in the conversation skills that union and management members needed to settle the terms of their relationship.

And hosting such conversations isn't a sideline to the church's central mission. As I noted in the first chapter, the Word created the human community; words continue to build or destroy it. Teaching our people how to talk well and providing good processes and healthy structured space for conversation is at the heart of what we are about.

The tools in this book are intended to help us talk together better. One of their characteristics is that they draw people together around questions rather than answers. This is easier to do when we remember that the "answer people"—the best theologians and politicians of the day—were the ones who condemned Jesus to death. Remembering the cross can help keep our conversation humble.

The church, unfortunately, has a reputation for delivering answers. Just walk into most sanctuaries. The seats are usually lined up so that everyone listens to one or a few people talk. There is no provision for participants to dialogue *with each other*. So when the church invites the community to a conversation, suspicion that the talk will be one-sided is a natural response.

One of my seminary interns, using the process described further on in this book, developed an interfaith group that invited the whole town to a conversation on the underemployment of young adults. At first there were almost no preregistrations, even though it had been determined that young adult unemployment was in fact a core concern of the community. People wondered what these churches were really up to. Finally, the group took out two full-page ads in the local paper. The ads explained why the churches were involved—that they were simply trying to host an open conversation, an asset-mapping exercise, about how to meet this employment need. Immediately after, the group was flooded with preregistrations. In the end they ran out of space.

Of course, many different organizations could host such a conversation. The church's gift may be that its concerns are inherently interdisciplinary, however, because as we have seen, God is concerned about the *whole* of life. Most of God's time is spent helping people balance checkbooks, make love to their mates, fix plumbing leaks, play video games, and design government policies. The church is no expert in these matters (and should make that clear). But the church does have a stake in ensuring that all life's slices work together in a way that reflects the wholeness of Trinity-shaped community.

Maze Walking

Churches can help people knit together lives fragmented by the bureaucratic mazes of modern society. I used to love mazes. Every winter when I was growing up, our local Mardi Gras featured an enormous straw-bale maze. I enjoyed racing my brother through it. Growing older, however, I've lost my enthusiasm for mazes as I've come to realize that I'm going to spend my entire life in one. Life in Canada and the United States is a bureaucratic maze. That's partly due to our wealth. Governments and organizations have the money to set up much-needed infrastructure: health care and justice systems; social welfare; water, power, and heat utilities; financial investment and lending structures; transportation and communication networks; and so on.

All that bureaucracy, however, creates a nightmare labyrinth for those who use the systems. Authorities must be approached at the right time and in the right order. Forms must be filled out correctly and computer software properly installed. Fees must be paid and decisions made on a schedule that is not always transparent. The requirements of one bureaucracy (such as health care) often compete with the requirements of others (such as Revenue Canada or the IRS). The maze of relationships is so complex that workers in one part of a system often don't know how they relate to workers in other parts of the same system. Small fiefdoms develop. They protect their turf from the encroachments of other clans at the expense of people who need coordinated service.

As citizens, we tend to be infantilized by this complexity. We end up trusting our lives to bureaucratic "parents," because we simply can't grasp all the regulations and procedures we are required to keep. We live in fear of the cascade effect. Having neglected one rule (for example, pay our income tax) we may find ourselves penalized (by fines) and unable to keep another (pay our utility bills). At worst, some people are completely overwhelmed and drop out, shunted to the sidelines of life, even to the streets. At best, all of us find ourselves at times deeply frustrated by the tortuous maze that modern life expects us to navigate.

These forms of social order are what I referred to earlier as God's way of governing the "flesh"—that is, the law in its civil use. The law helps to make relationships predictable through regulations and procedures that are agreed upon or imposed by those with power. The law in this sense derives from the capacity for order that God set into creation by separating light from darkness, sky from land, water from dry ground. Perhaps reflecting a love for ordered relationships within the Trinity, God's creation has the (God-given) capacity to organize its own life. So sodium ions form into salt crystals, birds build intricate nests, and humans create bureaucracies.

We see this dynamic at work early in Israel's life. In Exodus 18 Moses gets overwhelmed by the number of requests for conflict mediation being brought to him. His father-in-law, Jethro, suggests that Moses impose a judicial structure on the nation that would allow these disputes to be settled by local leaders and only taken to regional authorities or to Moses in the most serious cases.

As necessary and useful as civil law is, however, its codified forms are not adequate to handle all of life's infinite variety (although bureaucrats endlessly proliferate rules in the effort to do so). Real life requires a playful, inventive responsiveness. This creativity is not often nurtured in institutions but is still available to us. In fact, the capacity to create new forms of life, culture, and technology to meet changing circumstances is built into creation. It reflects God's own fertile imagination. But when we don't use that capacity, systems that were developed to sustain life can impede, complicate, or destroy it. Let me share a few examples from my own experience.

While I was in my second parish, a homeless man approached me and said that he wanted to get off the street. Bob said he'd been living outdoors since he was fourteen. But now he was forty and just couldn't handle shivering through the long nights in a cardboard box in minus forty temperatures anymore. He'd almost died from exposure the previous winter. He wanted to "get into the system," he said.

So we got started. Bob needed a place to stay. But that required a month's rent and a damage deposit (another month's rent) paid up front. Since he didn't have a credit record, he also had to pony up a deposit to each of the utilities he wanted to sign up for. To earn that money, he needed a job and someone willing to donate board and room for at least a month until he got his first check. For a job he needed a social insurance number. For a social insurance number he needed a birth certificate, which he didn't have. To get a birth certificate required finding a valid guarantor who could verify Bob's birth details.

On his own, with no knowledge of these systems and little education, Bob couldn't possibly have obtained these things. But I and a couple of others helped him obtain the keys to civil society. We put him up, researched his birth, and through our contacts with lawyers and others helped him get his papers, a job, and a place to stay.

Three months later Bob disappeared. I got a phone message shortly afterward. He apologized profusely, saying how much he appreciated our assistance. "I couldn't have gotten in without your help," he said. "But in the end it was just too much. Life in the system is way too complicated. I couldn't keep it up."

I had my own experience of that. In Africa I contracted a deadly parasite, which attacked the lining of my digestive tract. A friend woke me out of delirium, got me to a local doctor, and saw me onto my flight back to Canada. It was on that flight that the worst of the illness hit. For fifty hours, in the air and in airports, I endured a lot of pain and blood loss. Arriving in Toronto, I couldn't walk. Airline attendants shipped me in a taxi to a nearby hospital. The emergency ward had a long lineup for a computer-based triage. There were no wheelchairs and no waiting room attendants, no numbers were given out, and triage took about ten minutes per person. Only those patients who could stand in line for an hour or so could be assigned to the waiting room. The sickest ones (including me) never got to the front of the line. They had to leave.

I finally phoned a cab, which took me to a random hotel where I collapsed and slept for a day. Regaining a little strength, I flew home to Saskatoon. There I started into a ten-day round of travel back and forth several times between my doctor, the test dispenser, my home, and the pharmacist. A mistake was made, which required the whole sequence to be done again. At the end of it, the doctor said, "Whoever took you to that African clinic before you left saved your life. If it had been up to us, you'd be dead by now."

I discovered how very hard it is to navigate the maze of our health care system precisely at a time when one's resources are most depleted. Like the sick person at the pool of Bethzatha in John 5, I would never have been able to be healed unless a friend in Africa had helped me into the water (taken me to the clinic). Similar stories could be told of people entering our judicial, social welfare, and other systems, too. Those most in need are not able, by themselves, to access the benefits our complex bureaucracies are intended to distribute. The wealthy can hire helpers— lawyers, advocates, nurses, and so on—but others must fend for themselves.

In our social systems, the church has a wonderful opportunity to serve as the embodiment of the Holy Spirit. Jesus describes the Spirit as one who "comes alongside," one who *accompanies* those in distress (John 14:16)—the Paraclete or Advocate. If that is the Spirit's mission, it must surely also in some measure be ours.

However, maze walking as a ministry is different from the relief efforts churches tend to prefer. Congregations donate used clothes, overnight shelter, and meals to the homeless. But as I noted earlier, if you ask homeless people what they want, they usually say, "*Homes.*" How many churches are willing to engage the long and difficult work of helping homeless people find permanent rooms and adjust to living in them? How many lobby governments for single-tenant subsidized housing or organize it themselves? Such enterprises take long-term work. Churches love to fix problems and move on. But maze walkers are not fixers; they are *guides.*

Maze walking requires three skills or sets of tools: map reading, sending up flares, and a backpack and a rope.

MAP READING
It takes a bit of research to help an accused person find a good lawyer (pro bono needed for many).Walking with the chronically ill requires checking out hospital and care home procedures for admittance, visitors, handling prescriptions, and scheduling the

trips to various specialists. Families needing social welfare or multiple agency help may need assistance in figuring out their legislative rights and determining which things have to be done in what order.

SENDING UP FLARES

Often service providers don't recognize when those in need get lost in their systems. In part, that's because the need itself can be debilitating. Those who are ill often can't coordinate on their own the multiple trips, probing questions, and invasive tests that our health system requires. And sometimes those needing the service don't have the status, energy, education, or physical capacity to make their needs known. Companions can help attract the attention of maze managers. Often service providers simply don't know what effect their system is having on those who use it. After my wretched experience with the Toronto hospital, a friend urged me to write them a letter. I wasn't sure I wanted the hassle, but my friend persisted, so I wrote the letter. A few months later the director wrote back saying, "We thought we were losing people from the emergency ward. We just didn't know who or why. Because of your feedback, we've changed that triage system and reconfigured our emergency ward to be more hospitable." A problem that was obvious to patients was opaque to the health care providers. Churches can help people give feedback to institutions. They can help systems understand what works and what doesn't.

A BACKPACK AND A ROPE

Maze walking is not a commitment for the fainthearted. Once you're into a maze with someone, it's not always easy to get out. You may be in there for the long term. If so, you'll need to pack along patience, a willingness to do one's homework on the maps, and trust that God will use you effectively when you think you're doing nothing but getting your friend more desperately lost. It's best of all if you go in as a group. Tie yourself to partners in the congregation. As a congregation, link up with community organizations, self-help and advocacy groups, and well-placed friends in institutions. Walking together through the maze helps ensure that no one gets lost. And a congregation that partners with others builds its own maze-walking skills by learning from them.

The Rite Stuff

We need help navigating not only through our social systems but also through life crises and transitions. A couple of recent graduates from the Saskatoon Theological Union took adjoining parishes for their first calls just before two Mounted Police officers were shot and killed in that region. Families and friends of both the victims and the accused were members of their churches. These two pastors found themselves thrown into the local and national spotlight. They were expected to provide a way—a communal liturgy—for people to process the grief and horror of that experience. And that's what the pastors did. They created opportunities for folks to pray and lament. They modeled ways to be hospitable to media, to care for families. They helped their people channel the powerful but chaotic emotions triggered by the murders into a community-building experience. They mobilized hope and helped the region recover a view of itself as something other than a place that murders its police.

I experienced the power of community ritual when I attended a protest outside our local prison. Our correctional center is overcrowded and, in spite of the recommendations of a provincial audit several years ago, has very little programming. (It "keeps" but doesn't "correct.") It has become mostly a warehouse for the accused and convicted.

I arrived at the prison on a cold, dark fall evening. A group of thirty or forty were standing outside the razor-wire fence. I wasn't sure what to do. I'd come with lots of enthusiasm for the protest, only to realize when I got there that I didn't really know how to go about it. What do prison-reform protesters do? I soon found out. Most of the inmates in the prison are First Nations, so Native elders took charge. They gathered us into a circle and passed a smudge around. We waved smoke over ourselves and toward the prison as a sign of purification and protection. Candles were handed out and lit. One Native elder stood in the circle and shared her experience inside the prison; another did the same. Then an elder took up a drum and began to beat it steadily while prayers for reform were offered from several Christian and other faith traditions. The prayers weren't audible inside the prison, but I realized that the drum would be. The protest ended with a blessing for the prison and a challenge to those who run and fund it. That ritual shaped the evening into a powerful experience for us. It also created a vehicle to communicate hope to the prisoners, and through the media it conveyed a protest to the government.

Churches bring the rite stuff to their communities. Rituals—liturgies for life—give communities a way to celebrate (harvests or holidays) or lament (deaths and disasters). They provide a way to gather and share the stories of an era in the life of an individual or community (birthdays, anniversaries, commemorations). They help communities to begin things well (baptisms, weddings, the blessing of new buildings and officeholders) and end things well (farewells, closings). And rituals provide a process for healing and reconciliation from the conflict that a community inevitably suffers.

I mentioned earlier that one of my students created a liturgy for leaving the farm. That ritual helped to de-shame the leaving. It provided a way for healthy tears to mix with laughter in remembering. And it framed the leaving in a narrative of God's presence, shared suffering, and hope for the future.

Another student, recently graduated, saw his community faced with the closing of its kindergarten-to-grade-nine school. After participating in a creative and successful protest, the pastor asked the teacher of a grade four class for permission to help the students express their anxieties and thanksgiving. The teacher agreed. So the pastor showed the students a lament and thanksgiving psalm from the Bible and asked if they might write something similar about their experience of the school almost closing. Together they expressed their dismay and their joy in concrete, vivid lament language. That lament eventually went to the regional school board. It helped the board see the real, human impact of their decision, giving them a glimpse inside the children's hearts.

Liturgy—dramatic worship—comes naturally to the church because its life began in a drama: the story of creation leading to watery destruction, of Egyptian slaves becoming a Hebrew people, of exodus and exile, glory gained and lost, of hope hidden in humiliation and death. The biblical narrative has a plot and lots of action. It moves! And liturgy that flows out of that narrative moves too. When it's done well, liturgy moves people—moving their emotions, attitudes, and relationships from stuck to free, despair to hope, excluding to embracing, shame to honor, despised to beloved. Liturgy helps a community gather up the treasures of its past and let go of its accumulated trash. It propels a community into the future with confidence in the God to whom it belongs. And this is true even though not all who participate are people of religious faith. Good rites provide a way for a community to process common emotion; they engage the spirit of a place. Most community members can connect in some way to liturgies that are contextually sensitive.

Saving Grace

As a Lutheran I tend to think that one of the most important gifts we bring to the world is the gift of grace. Our theology divides God's providing, saving action in the world into two categories: law and gospel. Law takes several forms. I referred to its civil use earlier. Essentially law is about order and demand. Law constrains, guides, exposes. At its best, it directs us toward the healthy community life that the Trinity shares. At its worst, it traps us in structures that oppress and condemn us.

Law, unfortunately, has tended to be the church's favored tool. Whether because of society's expectation or the church's choice, congregations often assume the role of moral watchdog in their communities. This is revealed in the fact that people who get into deep moral difficulty, experiencing problems that are regarded as shameful (for example, adultery, bankruptcy, and drug addiction), tend to drop out of church. In their minds the church is a place where law-abiding folks go to hear about how to better abide by the law, how to be good people. Similarly, when Christian leaders break the law (crossing sexual boundaries, embezzling, beating their spouse, and so on), both the church and the nonchurch community are shocked. The assumption again is that the primary function of the church is to produce law-abiding people. So when Christian leaders sin publicly, hypocrisy is added to the charges against them.

However the law is useless, in fact oppressive, without the other gift God has given the church: the *gospel*. The gospel is God's *primary* gift. I express the good news this way: God says to us, "I am God. So *I* (not you) determine how you and I will be related. And I have decided that you are my beloved. I have shown you my love by sharing your life through Jesus, the Son. Because you are loved by me, you have enormous value. It's a value no one, not even you, can add to, and no one, not even you, can take away." The gospel is a word of *grace*. It says that our honor, our worth, our status are secure. There is nothing to be gained by fighting for control or by hiding our weaknesses. There is nothing to be lost by admitting our vulnerability or sin.

I said earlier that God's grace functions at a broad level in communities by ensuring that their future is not simply a reaping of what has been sown in the past but is truly open. Past conflicts, poor decisions, oppressive economic and political forces are not the final arbiter of a community's future life. To see how this is possible, however, it is helpful to note some of the ways in which grace operates within particular segments of the community and between individuals. Here are a few examples.

Grace is the foundation of true education. One teacher I know has a sign over her elementary schoolroom door that says, "This is a mistake-making place." Because human growth occurs primarily through struggle, a great number of mistakes must be made for any development to occur. If every mistake were a strike against us, if every error called into question our value and worth, we could never learn. Scientists would be unable to do experiments, fearing their hypotheses wouldn't be verified and their value as scientists would be called into question. No technological discoveries could be made. Truth is, human life from its earliest beginnings has been experimental. Only a deep undergirding of grace makes that possible.

Something similar can be said for other aspects of community life. If grace did not apply, people who are economically unproductive (those who are sick, unemployed, young, retired, or very relaxed) would quickly be cast aside. If grace were not operating, we would have little compassion for victims of globalization, terrorism, or climate change. They would have proven their unworthiness by their suffering. Grace brings dignity to those who suffer. When sufferers are valued, people care for them and thereby learn how to care for each other. Grace increases a community's resilience, its capacity to cope with crisis.

Grace also makes healthy, responsive government possible. A government that must pretend to be perfectly wise and capable in order to be honored among its citizens would avoid getting feedback from its people. Feedback could expose errors. Such a government could not have a genuine debate with opposition members, because the need to justify itself would override its desire to find out what is truly good for its people. It would inevitably be ineffective and corrupt.

If citizens had no sense of their intrinsic, God-given worth, they would be unable to spot evil, name it as such, and resist. The only determinant of a person's value would be the ability to wield power Nietzschean-style. In such a world, the strong—by definition—would be good; the weak would be bad. Social value would be demonstrated by the ability to control oneself, others, and one's environment—that is, not only by our ability to keep but also to *make* the law. In such a world, only the strongest would survive. As I've noted, that means eventually only *one* is left. Law on its own leads to the extinction of communities.

Finally, grace makes it possible for a community to get past blame and shame to see itself as it really is. At a conference of theologians in Wittenberg some years ago, German presenters said that in Germany after World War II, the government looked for culprits in order to punish them. This blocked the way to healing. In South Africa, they noted, leaders took a different direction. They looked for *truth*—not culprits. When grace leads, truth is possible. Where blame and punishment are paramount, there is no room for honesty and therefore no possibility of reconciliation or forgiveness.

And it is reconciliation, not retribution, that is truly liberating. Communities that punish their offenders do so hoping that fear of punishment will keep others from offending. They add a second harm to the first that was done, hoping that it will prevent a third from happening. But in my experience as a volunteer prison chaplain, most crimes are committed with very little awareness of potential punishment by the state. And now this second harm—the effects of imprisonment—also needs healing. The first victim's wound is not healed by wounding another. As someone said, "If our only response to harm is 'an eye for an eye and a tooth for a tooth,' we'd have a blind, toothless world."

Deep personal and social conflicts can only be dealt with by a cruciform grace that "does not hold our sins against us." Grace upholds the value of the *offender* and frees him or her from shame. *At the same time* it upholds the beloved status of the *neighbor*, the victim. Because both are beloved, grace insists, hostility between them is inappropriate. When offender and offended are free from the *need* to hate or ignore the other, reconciliation becomes possible (though never certain). Grace is the ground of love's compulsion to keep us connected even through sin and betrayal. Love, holding God together, was the Spirit's work at Calvary, when the Son cried to the Father, "My God, why have you forsaken me?" That same Spirit works to bind us, so that together we have to face the harm that's been done.

Unfortunately, reconciliation is very difficult in the case of criminal offense, because offenders and their victims are usually separated by our legal processes. Offenders rarely see the real effects of their crimes on victims. My son was stabbed and assaulted twice one year. His pastor invited him to tell the story of how that affected him to inmates and chaplains at our local prison. Afterward they said, "That's the first time we've heard a victim tell his story in here." It was deeply moving for all of them. Offenders therefore experience only the effects of *judicial* power on their *own* lives, not the impact they have had on their victims. Often they end up angry at and disaffected from the community that punishes them. Meanwhile victims are forgotten by society in its effort to convict and incarcerate offenders. Both victim and offender feel devalued.

But churches can help bring wholeness and reconnection. They do so first by explicitly, contextually *speaking* the gospel to both offenders and victims: "You are loved by God; you have enormous value. Nothing you've done, nothing that has been done *to* you, can change that." They also *walk with* both offenders and victims in their journey through legal systems. They offer the *liturgies* of confession and absolution. And they offer "enemies" a hospitable *space to talk* to each other, helping them struggle together through the issues or events that drove them apart. There is no guarantee, of course, that reconciliation will happen in any particular case. Grace must be grasped, forgiveness given.

Nonetheless, I believe that grace ultimately determines whether our struggles with each other will build community or destroy it. Because God has built *difference* into creation, struggle and conflict are essential to a community's growth. But people will stay in the wrestling match with each other over the long haul only if they know that both their own and the other's worth is secure. Knowing that—*no matter what*—I am God's beloved, and my neighbour is too, I can learn to love (or at least live with) my neighbor.

A Home Base

My experience of rural and inner city communities, where the majority of Canadian and American churches are located, is that they live with constant change. Rural areas often depend on one or two resources—minerals, crops, fish, livestock, lumber—that flourish and flop with the vagaries of international markets. Even tourist destinations wax and wane with the dollar's value. As a result, they experience a fairly high turnover of leaders and workers in basic community services. In inner city communities, urban "renewal" often has a similar effect, uprooting people from their homes and shattering long-established social structures. This is demoralizing to people who have worked for years to get a cultural or economic service going, only to see it dismantled when key leaders are forced to move out.

The problem is due in part to the fact that government planners tend to base their decisions on externals that are easy to see and measure—the condition of buildings, how much the government will have to pay per user to maintain the service, and so on. What governments have a much more difficult time measuring is *community capacity*—the network of trusting relationships, common history and shared experience, acquired skills and wisdom to apply all of these effectively to the unique context. The *inner* social infrastructure of a community is often invisible to decision makers. So with intentions of renewing, or at worst downsizing for greater efficiency, governments or the corporate industrial drivers of a region may rip apart the social net of a community, scattering its people and trashing decades of accumulated wisdom.

Rural and inner city congregations, of course, suffer from these changes along with other institutions. However, they usually have a denominational support system that is relatively independent of government and industry. Therefore many churches are able to endure in unstable communities when other institutions have folded.

As a result, their own institutional structure becomes a valuable resource in such places. Ed Chambers, an ex-seminarian who took over leadership of the Industrial Area Foundation (IAF) after founder Saul Alinsky died, saw the potential of churches as a resource for community organizing and development. Today more than sixty IAF groups are at work across the United States and now in Canada. They help community members band together across ethnic and denominational lines to tackle critical economic and social issues using local resources.

What Chambers realized was that churches can serve as excellent home bases for community building. There are several reasons:

1. *Almost all congregations own a building.* Granted, most sanctuaries are (unfortunately) not well designed for large group conversation. However, they are excellent

for presentations, and most churches have a basement
or fellowship hall where table groups can meet. Sunday
school rooms may serve for breakout groups or committee
meetings. There is usually a kitchen for food preparation,
washrooms, a heating and/or cooling plant, and so on.
Some (not nearly enough) are even handicapped accessible. Additionally, most have sound systems, projectors,
tables and chairs, art supplies, sports equipment, computers, and other basic tools essential to community-building
activity.

2. *Churches have at least one full- or part-time staff person
   who is trained in leadership development.* Clergy of most
   denominational stripes have at the center of their ministry
   the call found in Ephesians 4:11–12: Christ's gifts "were
   that some would be . . . pastors and teachers, to *equip
   the saints* for the work of ministry" (italics mine). While
   clergy in smaller congregations are constantly tempted
   to become the chief ministry-doers, they nonetheless
   recruit and train a significant number of leaders in every
   congregation for church council, Sunday school superin-
   tendent, committee chairs, altar guild, and so on. Church
   members are given regular opportunities for practice in
   public speaking, from giving announcements and reading
   at worship, to leading Bible studies, giving testimonials,
   and so on. Having leadership experience inside the church
   gives people confidence to take on similar roles in the
   community.

3. *Congregations have a fund-raising system.* People are
   used to giving regularly, not only to maintain the church
   organization but also to causes outside the church. A
   mechanism for collecting and accounting money is in
   place. Church people are used to being asked to contribute
   and budget personally for such contributions. Many are
   comfortable asking for gifts.

4. *Churches have a network of volunteers* who regularly offer,
   or are asked to offer, their time, experience, skills, and
   personal connections. Volunteers are used to starting

programs, attending and organizing meetings, laboring
without early rewards, evaluating what's been done,
and retooling. They are a tremendous gift to the larger
community.

5. *Churches have grassroots membership* and the respect
   of their communities. A church is one of the few places
   where people from a variety of socioeconomic groups are
   likely to interact with each other regularly. These are broad
   generalizations of course. They aren't true in the case of
   every particular congregation. But they are usually true of
   the churches in a community taken as a whole, which suggests that the community is likely to want to partner with
   them when they act ecumenically. A man who worked
   in Haiti after its devastating earthquake told me that the
   United Nations' convoys of food and medical supplies
   would have been relatively useless without the churches
   and long-term NGOs. They knew the people and had a
   social infrastructure that allowed help to be distributed
   where it was most needed.

6. *Most congregations are connected regionally, nationally, and
   globally* through their denominations. And most denominations boast a worldwide web of personal connections,
   information, tools, and even financial assistance to local
   congregations. They provide additional leadership training and access to support and advocacy groups of various
   kinds. Because of their involvement in their judicatories,
   congregations can be portals, opening a two-way flow
   between the community and the larger society. Denominations also often provide creative solutions to supply
   congregations with leadership even when the numbers are
   too small to warrant resident clergy.

7. *Churches are concerned for and talk about the well-being
   of their communities.* They have a language for discussing values, visions, and goals, and they use that language
   regularly in worship and small groups. Their challenge,
   of course, is to make sure that the language is fully accessible to those outside the church. We in the church could

drop most of our theological jargon. Too often it functions like the handles on Grandma's old trunk. We value the trunk. It is a symbol of our heritage. We know there are treasures inside, and so we use the theological handles to haul it from church to church and put it on display. But the truth is, we've forgotten exactly what is inside the trunk. Churches would do better to open those theological trunks, throw out anything that's rotten, dust off the true treasures, and give them away to their communities!

Overall, it's hard to quantify the contributions churches actually make to community development, but one small indication is the National Survey of Giving, Volunteering and Participating carried out in 2000 by Statistics Canada. It found that 41 percent of regular church attenders volunteered *in the community outside the church*, compared to 24 percent of those who were nonattenders. Regular attenders averaged 202 hours per year of community service (*in addition* to their work inside the church), compared to 149 hours for nonattenders.[13]

Undoubtedly, the church *is* engaging its community through the personal contributions of its members. Oddly enough, however, that contribution to community well-being is not well recognized as *the church's* contribution. For example, in the first decade of this century a multimillion dollar research project was carried out across Canada called the New Rural Economy. Excellent work was done on how rural communities develop social capital. But strangely, almost none of the researchers looked closely at the role of churches in developing community capacity.

That omission probably reflects a national blind spot that Canadians have, to go back to the discussion at the beginning of this chapter. But it may also reflect the failure of our churches to engage their communities *as churches* rather than just through the individual contributions of their members. In the next chapters we will look at how churches might go about this more intentionally.

CHAPTER 3

Appreciative Inquiry

Looking for God in the World

What causes a church or a community to change? One summer I gathered thirty-five people who were strongly connected in various ways to rural life and ministry—scholars, rural laypeople, rural clergy, aboriginal leaders, rural media, and others. We spent a couple of days telling stories and analyzing how community was being built in their rural and remote contexts. At the end, when we sorted out what was most essential for helping communities under stress, they said, "We need processes that help our people see themselves and their communities differently." *Seeing* differently, they insisted, is where we have to start. Churches can be like carnival goers in a house of mirrors. What they see is a distortion of who they really are. Often the mirror magnifies their struggles and losses and minimizes the work that God is really doing among them.

THE TRANSFORMATIVE POWER OF PERSPECTIVE

The process tools in this book help churches look at themselves in a new way. *Appreciative inquiry* can help us see God graciously at work among an imperfect people through a history pockmarked with scars and struggle. In *asset mapping* we discover that *all* aspects of our lives and our context, including our *weaknesses*, are resources for the Spirit to use in building community.

The power of new perspectives to change social structures has been well documented by sociologists. Pioneering American sociologists Peter Berger and Thomas Luckmann led the way with their 1960s book *The Social Construction of Reality*.[1] They insist that the shape and function of human organizations are *not* determined by natural laws that transcend contexts. Rather they are constructed and reconstructed by the people who live in them according to the beliefs and assumptions they negotiate in community relationships. Social structures are not ultimately at the mercy of inexorable trends or social principles. So there is hope for every community, every congregation, and every organization to reinvent itself.

Berger and Luckmann oppose a persistent tendency in research to assume that social order is something given to us in nature—a kind of ancient, underlying Jell-O mold into which we pour the particulars of our individual congregations and communities. It enhances the status of sociologists (myself included) if we can apply, universally, the social dynamics we discover in one context to all others. (For one thing, it creates a much bigger market for our books!)

But while any group of communities will have some features in common, overall, that sort of social stability really doesn't exist. For example, Canadians and Americans since the Second World War have lived with the nuclear family (mom, dad, son, and daughter) as a persistent, ideal, and "natural" social arrangement. However, even a quick glance at my Canadian prairie history shows that our people have been quite creative in their personal living arrangements. In the 1800s and early 1900s, prairie men worked the land with one family in the summer, then went north to lumber mills—and often to a second family—in the winter. The death of mothers in childbirth, and of men through accidents, was common. So children were often fostered out (Anne of Green Gables!) or, in the case of First Nations communities, were the responsibility of the whole community. And of course, around the world a variety of extended family arrangements have been typical, including polygamy and polyandry. Families have been headed by women as well as men. Power and authority has been concentrated in one person or divided according to family tasks. In North American cities today, single parenting and serial, same-sex, and common-law marriages often outnumber nuclear families.

Obviously, not every particular family arrangement, nuclear or otherwise, has worked out well for the particular people involved. But it illustrates that for good and for ill, humans have a capacity for creativity that extends not only to our technologies but also to our communal life.

The great historic variety in human social arrangements also reflects the biblical conviction that creation in general and humans in particular have been *created to be creative*. Theologians (like sociologists and perhaps all academics) enjoy analyzing and categorizing the world. They have gone to great lengths to describe the proper domains or orders within creation (such as economy, state, family). But the effort has tended to freeze the creative community-building process and privilege particular arrangements. "Orders of creation" doctrines tend to close down the future for a group or community by consigning them to an unbending fate. Such doctrines are popular with the most powerful because they justify racial, gender, class, caste, and other forms of oppression that concentrate power and privilege among those favored within each order (men in the family, for example, or corporations in the economic order).

But social life isn't a rigid set of categories. At its best it is a dance, a dynamic, constantly changing kaleidoscope of relationships, as a community creatively adapts to a changing environment and seeks new ways to create beauty, experience love, and enhance life. Our social creativity is easily constricted by narrow and myopic perspectives, however. Western Christian churches, for example, have shown a remarkable lack of imagination in dealing with the effects of rural-to-urban migration and economic change on congregational life. Old paradigms that envision a proper church as a pastor, a building, and a people to pay for them are well entrenched. But they induce despair in remote, First Nations, and inner city contexts, where money and educated clergy are hard to come by.

Seeing Is Doing

I once asked Carl Dudley, who perhaps more than any other had studied the small church in America, "What is the single most important factor in the vitality and renewal of small churches?" He responded immediately:

> It's their belief that vitality and renewal are possible. When churches think that their present course is the only one possible, they don't try to make changes. And when they don't try, nothing new happens. That reinforces their belief that nothing can be done to change it. It's a vicious circle.

Dudley makes a couple of critically important points here. First, he says that our perspective on our future tends to be self-fulfilling. Elijah's experience in 1 Kings is a great biblical example. Chapter 19 tells us that in spite of Elijah's best efforts to put on a convincing show for God at Mount Carmel, most of his congregation had gone over to the church of Baal down the street. Elijah was feeling lonely and discouraged. He figured that Yahweh's work in his town and his life was over, so he went out into the wilderness to die. He abandoned his people and his ministry. And Elijah would have died—except that God was there, sustaining his life with just enough food and water. Unfortunately, Elijah couldn't *see* that God was there, because he was looking for *big* signs, signs of power and success—earthquakes, wind, fire. Elijah assumed that our God is a *big* God and so would surely come to us in a big way.

Not until God helped him give up those assumptions and open himself to new perceptions did Elijah hear the divine voice, unexpectedly still and small. First God told Elijah that he wasn't alone. *God was there,* and when God is anywhere, with anyone, great things can happen. And second, God opened the blinders on Elijah's eyes. Perhaps Israel did not have as many believers as it once had. But there were still *seven thousand*; God had been sustaining the community, just as he had sustained Elijah. But Elijah had been counting only the losses, not those who had faith to share. When his perspective changed, his ministry was reborn.

Sometimes our small congregations think a lot like Elijah. They sink into a quiet depression. They may hope for a great sign of God's presence but don't really expect one. They hunker down and turn inward, eyes focused on their own survival. And in the process, they turn away from the community that needs them. They don't see those who would support them if they were only willing to look outward and ask.

But those that begin to see themselves and their future with new eyes tend to try new things. This is Dudley's second insight. Healthy change requires hope. Not every new thing that is tried will work, but *some* usually do. And in the process, congregations learn new skills, recharge their batteries, and gain a renewed vitality in their ministries.

Seeing from Below, Above, and Out Front

In his book *Hope within History*, Walter Brueggemann goes beyond asking *how* change begins to ask, "*With whom* does it begin?" He notes, "People excessively committed to present power arrangements and present canons of knowledge tend not to wait expectantly for the newness of God."[2]

Ben was the manager of a large agricultural business that was expanding rapidly. But his community was being devastated by depopulation due to the large-scale industrial farming from which Ben was profiting. He said to me, "Well, I think that in any part of our world, there are people or organizations that can be unjust, but . . . I can't see that the whole system can be unjust itself." Brueggemann is right: it's hard to bite the hand that feeds you.

Perhaps, then, it is those who are *struggling* who are more likely to look for change. Martyred theologian Dietrich Bonhoeffer first described what has come to be known as the "hermeneutical privilege of the oppressed." He suggests that those who are disadvantaged by any social arrangement are likely to see the problems in that system most clearly, because they are feeling the pinch. In one of his entries in *Letters and Papers from Prison*, Bonhoeffer writes that after the failure of German theology to prevent, or even critique, the horrors of the Second World War, "there remains an experience of incomparable value. We have for once learnt to see the great events of world history from below, from the experience of the outcast, the suspects, the maltreated, the powerless, the oppressed, the reviled—in short from the perspective of those who suffer."[3]

In my experience, however, the view from below is not always liberating. Certainly the shape of the problems is clearer when seen from below. But that view is often tinted with despair. I have recently been doing some work with young prisoners. In our setting, the majority are aboriginal people whose families have experienced social marginalization for generations. Many of them are from the urban poor, with limited education, little ambition, and a history of abuse and addiction. They can describe the things they struggle with but often see no way out. Listening to them has been a profound education for me. I've learned a great deal about how our corrections system doesn't work: that it warehouses but doesn't "correct." For my part, as a middle-class, educated clergyman, I've tried to offer these young adults support and the opportunity to imagine a different way of living. I try to help them imagine a world in which they have full access to the benefits of life in Canada. But I'm not very successful at it. It's difficult for these young offenders to hope. They struggle with long-entrenched habits, unhealed wounds, fragile support systems, a sense of being trapped under the weight of their past.

Change, then, doesn't necessarily begin with either those who see from above or those who see from below. Our social location gives us a certain interpretive advantage, but each location has significant limitations. That, of course, reinforces my conviction that congregational and community revitalization must begin with conversation among a broad spectrum of members. But there is one essential perspective that no members can supply, individually or even together. That's the view that comes from out front, from the future, from the standpoint of the risen Christ.

What do I mean by that? The execution of Jesus of Nazareth was a horrifying example of a fairly common occurrence under Roman rule in the first century. Mass crucifixions, in the hundreds and even thousands, were routine. The Romans used this barbaric form of death as a sentence for those accused (not always convicted) of treason. The victim's suffering was public, and lingering. Crucifixion was intended to shame and humiliate the executed. But even more, it was designed to breed *despair* in the bystanders—to force the population into submission by removing any hope that they might someday be free of Rome's oppressive rule. Jesus's family and friends lived in a society that had a long history of being trampled underfoot by larger powers. When Jesus became another victim of that oppressive pattern, his followers had good reason to despair.

What changed their perspective was the action of God. Raising Jesus from the dead was a surprising act, astonishing. There was no precedent for it. It was something genuinely new, completely unexpected. They came to see it as a gift from a future they couldn't have imagined, a down payment on a new life yet to come. As the risen Christ broke bread with them, he also broke the chains of despair in which they were bound by their personal and national past.

The resurrection of Christ reveals one of the mind-altering properties of the Bible. It twists our perspective on time. The Bible allows us to see the future not simply as pushed forward by the past ("reaping what we sow"), but as a gift sent to us from up ahead ("a foretaste of the feast to come"). Not only the risen Christ but also the prophets before and after him present the future as something new called into being by God. It supports John Haught's claim that time is a river in which we are standing, facing *upstream*.[4] The past is behind us, flowing away. The future is flowing toward us full of unpredictable possibilities.

It's important, however, that the Bible sees the future as *called* into being. The future is not engineered, delivered to us by God as a fait accompli. That would just turn it once again into *fate*, into something inevitable. We would be no more than passive observers, along for the ride. Rather, God stands upstream ahead of us, calling us, encouraging us to link hands as we wade through the rapids, to dodge the driftwood that appears suddenly around the corners, to learn to navigate the future together. Being able to face the future knowing that it is both a creation of our choosing and the work of a loving God is a gift of divine grace.

Grace as the Freedom to See the Future with New Eyes

God's grace opens the future for congregations and communities in three ways: First, *God graciously forgives their past and enables them to forgive each other.* I've observed several congregations that have fractured over conflicts. The fractures tend to grow as resentment leads to slights and new injuries. People's memories become crowded with grievances. The ability to imagine and create a future together fades into despair. When people hurt each other, the memory of the injury binds their behavior into an ongoing reaction to the pain. It limits options for action and relationships. In my experience, this vicious cycle can be interrupted only by an intentional, congregation-wide process of reconciliation, including honest listening, confession, and forgiveness. Forgiveness is a kind of release. Forgiveness lets go of the hurt. Forgiving, we allow the pain to dissolve into our lives, freeing us from its power so that we can live into an open future.

Forgiving each other begins with God forgiving us. God forgives, in part, for the same reason that we need to forgive each other. Because God gets hurt. The cross is the most potent and visible example of God's pain. But surely *any* injury in creation must be felt by God because in creation and incarnation the Three open themselves, become vulnerable to the experience of every particle in the universe, including each loss of love and beauty, every betrayal, sorrow, and death. God could be bound by that inconceivable pain into an eternity of judging and punishing. This is an image of God that is quite popular in our own and many cultures. In a perverted way, it serves our own god complex, because it makes us the puppet masters, jerking God about on the strings of our sin.

Instead God forgives. Why? To be the *God* of creation. God is not *God* if God's actions are simply *reactions* to the pain given by creation. Father, Son, and Spirit intend to *initiate* the relationship between us. So they choose to maintain not only an intense connection to creation (immanence), but a profound *freedom from* creation (transcendence) as well. They choose to coax creation into their own image in spite of creation's sin, death, and entropy. So God forgives the hurt, absorbs it, and lets it go. As a result, God is not bound to cope with our past sin or failure by dealing us a future dark with judgment.

Jesus demonstrates God's freedom in the Garden of Gethsemane (Matt. 26). He is confronted by a rabble of mercenaries hired by the chief priests and elders to arrest him. At that point Jesus has three options: fight, flee, or stay and take the pain. The first two options mean abandoning the mission—giving up on his beloved people. One of Jesus's followers opts to fight. Swinging his sword at the high priests' slave, he slices off the slave's ear. But Jesus rebukes him: "Do you think that I cannot appeal to my Father, and he will at once send me more than twelve legions of angels?" (v. 53). Jesus had the power to protect himself from or to take revenge on his assailants. Both actions would have diminished him and ultimately harmed those he loves. He chooses instead to absorb the hurt and forgive them. ("Father, forgive them; for they do not know what they are doing," he says in Luke 23:34 to his crucifiers).

This absorbing, however, is not simply passive acquiescence to evil. In the power of the Holy Spirit, Jesus is raised. The hopelessness that evil engenders is *overcome*. Jesus's resurrection is God's gracious signal that death and judgment are not the default future for humanity. (Nor is entropy the default future for creation.) Like the Easter tomb, our future has been broken open by the risen Christ.

Second, *God's forgiving grace frees us from our past.* The perspective the early disciples had as they stood "out front" with the risen Christ transformed their prior experience of the cross. They discovered that *God* had been present there "reconciling the world to himself," as Paul says in 2 Corinthians 5:19. That discovery took them out of their depressed huddle in the upper room. They became a people with a future, women and men on a mission. Because if God could be present in the violence of the cross, God can be at work in anyone, in any happening, anywhere, no matter how hopeless or horrible it might seem.

That same perspective can change a congregation or community's view of its own past. They may find the courage to look for the hidden work of God in the dark closets of their history. Unexpectedly, they may discover God was there in the fight over worship styles that split the church or in the city council's decision to tear down all the low-income housing to make room for condos or in the closing of the copper mine. These darkest periods, in fact, can become the times most transparent to divine activity. Because when human resources fail, the acts of honest communication, courage, persistence, mutual care, and empowerment that nonetheless emerge to make survival possible are more easily seen to be the work of God.

When a community or congregation can see the presence of God in its history, shame and regret lose their hold the people's spirit. God's presence reveals that this is a group God values, people worth standing by. So their past is changed. Their identity is transformed. They cease to be those who failed and were forsaken. Now they are a people who struggled but were accompanied by the sustaining power of God.

When shame is removed, it is much easier to forgive each other. Seeing the miracle of God's grace in the darkest moments of our past frees us from having to control or repay others in order to guarantee a good future. We can see that the hurts we inflict on each other have not—and *cannot*—devalue us or destroy our future. Our value, and our future, belong to *God*, who has chosen to stick with us no matter what.

Third, *God opens the future for a community by graciously "putting the people on."* The phrase is awkward, but it's the best I can find to describe the way the term *charisms*—gifts of grace—is used in the New Testament. There are several lists of these gifts of grace: 1 Peter 4, Romans 12, Ephesians 4, and 1 Corinthians 12 are a few. They include as charisms everything from everyday activity ("administering") to benevolent behavior ("giving"), to personality traits ("cheerfulness"), to roles ("pastors and teachers"), to ecstatic experience ("speaking in tongues") and plain communication ("speaking"). Apparently, *all* that we are can become a gift of grace in the hands of the Spirit.

I imagine it this way: the Spirit enters a congregation or community and *puts it on*—like a glove. All that those people are—their history, personality, resources, *even weaknesses*—becomes a tool of the Father, Son, and Spirit for building a God-shaped community. Worn by the Spirit, filled with the Spirit, they accomplish more than one could expect, given their history. In fact, their weaknesses become their greatest witness (see 1 Cor. 1:26–31). I'll say more about this in a later chapter. But simply, when a glove has holes in it, everyone can see the hand inside that moves the glove. It's clear that the glove is not acting autonomously out of its own power. When our weaknesses are used by God to build community, the world is able to see that *God* is at work.

Appreciative inquiry, asset mapping, and intergenerational dialogue can function, almost sacramentally, as vehicles for the experience of grace that I have described. They help to develop a people's skills in

- *affirmation:* the ability to *see God at work* in their past, even its darkest moments, and affirm that work and their own value to God as a community.
- *generation:* the ability to *imagine a future* with God that is open and full of possibilities that they can realize using their own resources.
- *collaboration:* the ability to *work together* to build a Trinity-shaped community.

SEEING THE WORLD THROUGH THE EYES OF APPRECIATIVE INQUIRY

Appreciative inquiry is a process designed by David Cooperrider and Suresh Srivastva in the late 1980s. They wanted to help organizations grow by focusing on what had been *working* in the organizations' past, rather than by analyzing what had gone wrong. They then used those discoveries as a springboard for imaginative planning.[5]

Appreciative inquiry has been adapted to a variety of uses and disciplines. It is not so much a single method (step 1, step 2, step

3) as a perspective or approach to dealing with life. The Clergy Leadership Institute (see their website at www.clergyleadership. com) offers a wonderful set of resources for applying appreciative inquiry principles to various aspects of church ministry, personal spirituality, organizational planning, and relationships in general.

The church, however, walks a perilous path when it adopts any perspective or process without first asking how it may or may not serve the gospel. The fact that something works—is effective, powerful—has little to do with whether it suits the church's gospel mission.[6]

The usefulness of appreciative inquiry to the mission of the church depends in part on the particular questions in the inquiry. To be *appreciative*, they must be questions that look toward the positive. But to be questions arising out of faith, they must look in some way for the positive action of *God* in the world.

I said in the previous chapter that one of the gifts churches can give to their communities is "head space." Appreciative inquiry done out of a faith context opens up head space in a couple of ways: first, by opening people to the action of God even in the dark places of their past, as I've said; and second, by helping them discover some meaning and purpose in their common (in the sense of both corporate and ordinary) life.

It seems that Americans are in hot pursuit of life's meaning. For example, a 2004 national survey of more than 112,000 college freshmen by the Higher Education Research Institute at UCLA found that 80 percent have an interest in spirituality, 74 percent talk about the meaning and purpose of their life with friends, and 69 percent pray. Apparently, even the most educated in our high-tech, secular societies veer away from the stark despair of renowned atheist Bertrand Russell, who wrote in 1918:

> Brief and powerless is Man's life; on him and all his race the slow, sure doom falls pitiless and dark. Blind to good and evil, reckless of destruction, omnipotent matter rolls on its relentless way; for Man, condemned today to lose his dearest, tomorrow himself to pass through the gate of darkness, it remains only to cherish, ere yet the blow falls, the lofty thoughts that ennoble his little day;

disdaining the coward terrors of the slave of Fate, to worship at the shrine that his own hands have built.[7]

Honest as it is, Russell's cynicism leaves little motivation for building relationships or pursuing dreams. Yet in the intensity of his writing one can sense a heart that yearns for meaning in spite of his conviction that there is none.

Building *meaning-full* community and dreaming dreams is what appreciative inquiry is all about. It does so by asking four kinds of positive questions. The particular questions must be adapted to suit the context, but they fall into four broad categories: peak experience, core values, hopes, and commitments.

Peak Experience questions ask, What has been good, and of God, in our past? Here, of course, the term *good* has to be fleshed out. Kelly Fryer, a church consultant, assumes that *courage*, stepping out in faith, is good. So she asks individuals and congregations, "What is the most daring thing that you have done?" As they talk about their acts of daring-do, it becomes easier to see themselves as risk takers, ready to take on something new.

In the first chapter, I identified some core dynamics of a trinitarian community. Though these are intended more as background principles for selecting good community-building processes, they could also be put into concrete question form. So one could ask about positive experiences of *difference*: "Tell me about a time when your feelings about worship changed because you listened to someone else talk about *their* preferences." Or one could ask about *distributed power*: "Tell about a time when you felt you were able to provide significant input into the decision making in this church (or community)." Or one could simply ask the more general question, "Tell about a time when you felt that God was at work in this place."

Core Values questions ask, What do we value most about our congregation or community? This question helps participants express for themselves what they find to be good about their congregation or community. "What do you value most about the young people in this town?" "What difference do they make in your life?" One rural church that did an appreciative inquiry was being pressured by some members to close its doors. They couldn't afford a pastor and a building. But as they told each other their stories of what they had valued about that church, the Sunday school kept coming up again and again. They realized the children's ministry was something really good they had to offer their community. So they didn't close. And recently one of the members phoned me and said, "You know what's happened? We've been contacting young families in the area, and our Sunday school is growing. People are starting to give generously again. We've got a new lease on life!"

Hopes questions ask, What do we wish for? Questions in this category help people use their responses to the previous questions as a springboard for imagining the future. For example, "So, you had a great time with those kids when you went fishing together. And you said you really value their enthusiasm for life and the opportunity to share some of your skills with them. Now if you had three wishes for your (or the church's) relationship with them in the future—and there were no restrictions—what would you wish for? And how would you or our church or our community be different if those wishes came true?"

Commitments questions ask, What would you be willing to offer (time, personality, things you could give or lend, skills, experience, connections, and so forth) to help that wish come true? I like to explore this question in a group format using an asset-mapping exercise, which I will describe in the next chapter.

ASSUMPTIONS OF APPRECIATIVE INQUIRY

Questions such as those above are not neutral (if any questions are). They are embedded in a web of assumptions about how communities grow and function. The most basic assumption for those who use appreciative inquiry in a faith setting is, as is obvious from the preceding discussion, that *God is at work for good in every person and community at all times*. But appreciative inquiry includes additional assumptions about human nature and organizations, as follows:[8]

- The way we see ourselves is the way we will act.
- Our self-image is determined by the questions we ask.
- Like plants, people tend to grow toward the light.
- To move into the future with confidence, we need to take the best out of our past.
- We have to work together.

The Way We See Ourselves Is the Way We Will Act

If we see ourselves as a problem congregation, we'll be one. This is the self-fulfilling aspect of social perspective mentioned above. If we see ourselves, and *talk* about ourselves, as a congregation that works, then we'll become a congregation that works. If we say, "We're *just* a small church" or "We have *only* thirty people at most in worship" or "We *can't* afford to do much" or "We *used* to have a great Sunday school," we paint our future as a dark tunnel with no light at the end. Who wants to do something new if there is no future? But congregations that say, "We really know each other well and care for each other" know they have a gift that can be shared and developed.

Appreciative talk doesn't mean that we deny our problems. It is simply a way of recognizing that humans tend to live within norms. If I think I'm a hopeless wreck, I'm not likely to make much of an effort to change; I assume that the effort will be wasted. If I see myself as a basically a healthy kind of guy, then I'm more likely to eat good food and exercise. If a community comes to see itself as a place that normally cares for the elderly, then—*no matter how much they actually do care for the elderly at present*—elder care is likely to take a more prominent place in their planning for the future.

One of my interns did an appreciative inquiry in a suburban church looking at the impact of ministry by youth on the congregation. Her opening question was, "Tell me about a time you recall when the youth of the congregation made a positive impact on you personally or the general life of the congregation." She said that as they told stories in response to that question, the congregation became aware of themselves as a place that valued young people. Immediately after the inquiry, two church committees invited youth to participate in their meetings and began to provide prayer and financial support for youth projects. The deacons invited youth to write three of the devotionals in the Advent devotional booklet they were preparing for the congregation. The intern said, "Rather than bemoaning the lack of youth involvement in the life of the congregation, people were taking action and inviting youth to be involved in their area of ministry." Youth also responded to the inquiry. Instead of sitting in the back rows and heading off to the youth room as soon as the service ended, they began to engage congregation members in conversation and took leadership at six Sunday services. The intern concluded, "There was an awakening of the things they share, belonging to the same congregation, believing in the same God. Out of this realization came the openness to be in ministry together."

Our Self-Image Is Determined by the Questions We Ask

The intern in the example above said she quickly became aware that "what gets talked about gets noticed." And what gets noticed gets action. Cooperrider claims that organizations grow in the direction of their most frequently asked question. If we are constantly asking, "What's wrong with the youth in this town?" the youth and their problems will occupy our attention and energy. We'll become experts on youth problems. If we are constantly asking, "How is it that some of our youth have become community leaders?" we'll become occupied with examining the factors that lead to healthy, productive youth.

Of course, as we focus on youth leadership, for example, other people and issues will tend to fade into the background. So the questions we ask reflect *choices* we make. We choose whether to focus on problems or solutions. (Appreciative inquiry favors the latter.) And we choose which *aspect* of our communal life to focus on.

Like Plants, People Tend to Grow toward the Light

Generally, hope is a better long-term motivator than fear. Fear tends to have a short horizon. It drives us away from the things that dissatisfy and hurt us. But once we've got a little distance, we stop moving. So fear can arouse energy for action, but the energy dissipates when the worst of the crisis is over. At best, fear-based action can lead only to a life with less discomfort—a neutral life, but not a life filled with meaning. In fact, it leads to an existence more like death than life.

Hope, on the other hand, draws us toward the things that satisfy us, that make life whole and good in the long term. My wife and I discovered the importance of "satisfiers" as our children left home. We decided to build a new house. It has lots of labor-saving devices and is relatively free of the pain of noisy, messy children. But it turns out that quiet cleanliness doesn't fill the soul like the love and laughter that our children bring.

It must be said that fear often disguises itself in the language of hope. We say, "I hope they'll get rid of those drug dealers down on Seventh Street." But disposing of the drug dealers does not give that community any idea as to what might be a better use of Seventh Street.

Churches also confuse fear with hope when they speak about salvation only as *deliverance*—usually from sin, death, and hell. God could easily fulfill such a hope for us simply by ending our existence: salvation as obliteration. True hope looks for the fulfillment of life, not the avoidance of pain and suffering. And so a biblical hope clings to the images of the new Jerusalem and the new creation, saturated with the presence of God, the nations sharing their gifts with each other, the lion lying down with the lamb.

By focusing on best practices and that which people value (the satisfiers), appreciative inquiry moves people toward a positive future, while at the same time (almost as a side effect) moving them away from that which detracts from life.

To Move into the Future with Confidence, We Need to Take the Best Out of Our Past

Appreciative inquiry is one tool in a group of social tools that overall might be called *solution focused* rather than *problem focused*. Therapists have begun to focus on coping strategies that, at least to some extent, are already at work in the lives of distressed patients.[9] Government agencies are starting to examine what their civil servants are doing that might constitute *best practice*.[10] Some schools and businesses are approaching change by looking for *positive deviants* in their organizations. These are people who are moving against the flow; they are functioning well in a context in which most are struggling. Finding the "deviants" and helping them articulate how and why they are able to do well makes their wisdom and skill available to the whole group.[11]

Appreciative inquiry assumes that simply becoming aware of *how much* actually is working—and *why* it's working—builds community members' ability to imagine themselves in a more positive future. Focusing on the (often vast) extent of a problem tends to erode that ability. So appreciative inquiry mines people's memories for evidence of movement in the direction of their mission. That evidence gives them courage to try something new again. And it yields some hints as to where they might begin. The memories become a springboard for confident new action.

We Have to Work Together

No one leader can tell us which direction to take. Therefore, in appreciative inquiry many members are interviewed. Each tells his or her story of what has worked, what matters most, what he or she hopes for. It takes broad input and commitment for the full resources of a congregation or community to be uncovered and mobilized. And the partners that a congregation might enlist are as broad as the community.

In my experience, churches have a tendency to think of partnership only within their denomination, or even within their congregation. But the town council, local schools and businesses, faith communities of various stripes—all those groups and institutions in the community are potential partners.

The depth of the partnership will vary, of course. Partnerships are almost always limited in some way. But points of connection between a congregation's mission and the basic goals of other groups and institutions usually can be found, allowing them to work together in those areas.

In its workbook *Building Strategic Partnerships to Foster Inclusion*, the Corporation for National and Community Service identifies four levels of partnership: (1) Most partnerships may simply involve *communication*—sharing information, keeping in touch; or (2) there may be *coordination* to ensure that services are not duplicated and gaps are filled; (3) *cooperation* suggests a willingness to integrate some operations without sacrificing each group's autonomy; and (4) *collaboration* is when partners commit themselves fully to working together on a common goal, even at some cost to their individual organizations.[12]

THE POWER OF GOOD QUESTIONS

I want to look more closely at the basic assumption that *questions* (inquiry) asked in an *appreciative* (positive) way have such power to change a community's practices. I'll look first at the power of questions, and then I'll ask whether an appreciative approach really fits with our understanding of the brokenness of human life (the doctrine of original sin).

Questions are essentially research strategies. They outline what a congregation or community wants to know about itself and, by implication, what its possibilities are. Bad questions shut out critical information—or even misinform. In my Introduction to Theology class, I ask students to bring me a good question three times during the semester. They usually struggle with this. The first questions handed in tend to be rhetorical—comments disguised as questions. They might ask, "Why is Lutheran worship so boring?" or "Why don't we talk more about the Holy Spirit?"

Their questions eliminate the possibility that Lutheran worship *isn't* boring to others, even if it is to them, or that Lutheran discussions about the Holy Spirit are going on that they have missed out on. They assume facts not in evidence. Their questions are really just opinions looking for justification.

Either-or options are also common: "Did God create human beings or did evolution?" No matter how many real possibilities there are, these black or white questions reduce the field of possible options to only two, one of which is usually obviously preferred. (But maybe it was both God *and* evolution—or aliens!) Either-or questions contain embedded assumptions about what the range of answers to the question can be.

Yes-no questions aren't particularly useful because they can be answered in one word. Appreciative inquiry tries to get at people's *stories*. So the questions need to be open-ended. Don't ask, "Is our community in good economic shape?" but "Tell about a time when you saw this community doing something effective to strengthen its economy."

My theology students' questions may also be diversions away from the concerns that matter most to them but are a bit scary to consider. "What if God doesn't exist?" may be sidestepped by someone training to spend his or her life telling people about God in favor of "Is it okay to let unbaptized people come to communion?" Diversion questions often pop up in congregational debates. For several years many of our Canadian rural churches have been heatedly debating whether they should be blessing same-sex marriages—even in tiny communities where there are no gay or lesbian couples interested in marriage. Meanwhile, economic changes that are depopulating those communities and dismantling their social infrastructure go unquestioned. Energy that should be devoted to building communities under stress is going into fighting an issue whose resolution will have little or no impact on their particular community, *no matter how it is resolved.*

So bad questions can distort a congregation's self-image, limit its options for action, and divert it from exploring the things that matter most. Good questions give them confidence in themselves, open up their future, and get at the heart of their community's needs.

Jesus had a gift for spotting bad questions. His detractors were always trying to trap him with questions: "Who sinned, Rabbi: this man or his parents?" (The question assumes that all bad events are a result of personal sin, which, considering the unfortunate series of circumstances in Jesus's life, would have branded Jesus a major league sinner.) "Should we pay taxes to Caesar?" ("Yes" would have put Jesus in trouble with his oppressed fellow Israelites; "No" would have had him in trouble with Rome.) One of my favorites, though, is the apparently innocent question asked by the lawyer in Luke 10:29: "Who is my neighbor?" If Jesus had answered this question, he would have been forced into outlining criteria as to who deserved the lawyer's care. The question, Jesus realized, was the lawyer's way of protecting his present lifestyle by implying that there were those who *didn't* deserve his help. The lawyer wanted to avoid change yet obtain the approval of God.

Instead of answering directly, Jesus tells the parable of the good Samaritan. Then he ends with a reversed question: "Which of these three, do you think, *was a neighbor* to the man who fell into the hands of the robbers?" Now it is not the worthiness of others that is in question but the lawyer's *willingness to help them, regardless of who they are.* Jesus's question reveals God's indiscriminate love at work in one whom the lawyer would normally have despised. It opens up the possibility that the lawyer's careful retirement plan— what he had to "do to inherit eternal life" (v. 25)—might need to be drastically altered.

Good questions are also an effective way of mobilizing community energy. A leader who provides *answers* out of his or her personal vision has to do a lot of work to get others to sign on. Even then, people's buy-in may be halfhearted. But good *questions* arouse the interest of people, who find themselves exploring their own and others' stories. In the process they will begin to formulate their own answers (to which they are much more likely to be committed) and will begin forging connections that can serve as the nucleus of an action team.

Drafting appropriate questions within the four general areas described above is actually one of the more difficult aspects of conducting an appreciative inquiry. Here are some suggestions. First, select an area of inquiry that *matters* to your people. Sit down with several church and community people who are likely to see the community from different perspectives: for example a bartender, town councilor, teacher, policeman, welfare client, nurse, clergy, ex-con, and so on. Ask them, "What is happening in this town, or not happening, that is having a significant impact on our people?" Allow each to share in turn, and use their responses to focus on an area of interest that you want to pursue in an appreciative inquiry.

Then draft one main question for each of the four areas listed above: that is, best experience, core values, hopes, and commitments. A main question under best experience might be, "Tell about an experience you've had when you saw this community doing something effective to strengthen its economy," or "Tell about a time when our church did something effective with our community's youth."

You will also need to prepare supplementary subquestions to draw out the person's response to the main question, so to follow up on the economic question above, one might ask, "*How* did that approach (project, experience) strengthen our economy?" "*Who* was involved, and *how* did they get involved?" "*Why* did it work?" "*Where or when* have you seen that same approach used again?" and so on. Generally, the who, what, where, when, why, and how questions open up the conversation best. "Tell me about a time when . . ." is good for getting stories started. "Give me an example . . ." gets into important contextual details. "How did you feel when . . . ?" helps to expose the storyteller's core values. Avoid either-or questions or any that begin with the words *do* or *does*, *will, can, should,* or *is,* which normally lead to yes or no or very brief responses. See appendix A for some examples of questions that could be used in various areas of a church-community appreciative inquiry.

Using Good Questions: An Appreciative Inquiry on Youth and Worship

Here is an example that illustrates how appreciative inquiry questions might be used: One of our seminary's interns did an appreciative inquiry in a small rural community in which its young people, parents, and youth leaders tried to get at what it is that feeds their spirituality. The interviews were carried out in a small group format. She asked them to discuss and take notes on the question, "What makes you feel closer to God? Tell about a time when you felt connected to God." Her subquestions were "What parts of our present church service or existing tradition feed you?" "When has your life had deep meaning?"

Participants told a wide range of stories about holy times and places: attending a funeral with its deep emotions and spiritual significance, a candlelight service at Christmas, sitting on a mountaintop in Austria, meeting God in a time of serious illness, the arrival of a new child in the family, and more.

As the group began to get excited about these stories of holy moments, she helped them identify their core values, asking, "What do you really value in worship?"[13] Again, responses varied: loud singing, quiet reflection, vivid sermons, incense, Easter blessings, involving other cultures (for example, a Mexican Lutheran service), spontaneous prayer, lots of instruments, circular seating, meditation in the outdoors, and so on.

She then asked them to paint a picture of a worship experience they might hope for, asking where and when it would be, what they might be doing, and who would be leading. So they dreamed concretely about keeping an online devotional connection with each other during the week, offering multidenominational youth worship, increasing the amount of teaching in the services, moving services outdoors at certain times and seasons, bringing in guest leaders and involving more people in worship leadership, providing a worship experience that was "progressive"—one that moved from place to place like a traveling supper—and so on.

Finally, with a small group of youth, parents, and leaders, she pulled together several provocative possibilities out of the input that had been given, brought them back to the larger group, and asked what they might be willing to commit to. In the end, they decided to hold two outdoor services in the summer that would be visible to and welcoming of the community and would incorporate visible symbols but less paper, spontaneous sermons and stories, and popular music. Two teams were organized to plan and lead the two services.

The student reported that the events themselves were a wonderful experience. But even better were the connections made during the process itself. People became aware of differences in spiritual preferences between genders and age groups in that congregation. People young and old with gifts in music and leadership came out of the woodwork. Treasured hymns and liturgical pieces were identified. The process stirred up interest in attending conferences on worship in other places. Relationships between generations and denominations were forged and strengthened.

Appreciative Inquiry and Original Sin

The second core element that needs to be examined is the "appreciative" aspect of the inquiry. I've heard theologians say they are not sure appreciative inquiry takes original sin seriously enough. They are concerned that appreciative inquiry questions don't inquire into the nature and causes of the brokenness in creation. By original sin, I am referring to that complex of personal and societal habits, genetic inheritance, social and economic structures, and broken relationships that tend to trap humanity in behavior that is destructive to themselves and others. Appreciative inquiry can seem to ignore these hard realities in favor of spiritual denial. It may look like a recycling of Norman Vincent Peale's old classic, *The Power of Positive Thinking.*

However, it is important to remember that doctrines like that of original sin function differently in different contexts. They are not passive truths disconnected from real life. In a setting where the sense of loss, social trauma, or corporate depression is profound (for example, in decaying inner cities, dying suburbs, stressed rural communities), people already have an overly strong sense of the forces that bind them, that are sucking them dry. They feel like a fly caught in a spider's web. For them, the doctrine of original sin simply reflects and reinforces their sense of hopelessness. What they need is to be freed to imagine and act differently. They need to know that God is greater than the forces that bind them. And appreciative inquiry can help with that.

There are certainly times, however, when speaking to powerful people and organizations, that it is critically important to point out how their actions are hurting others. Change, as I've noted, isn't going to happen when people don't realize there is a need for it. Those who already have an arrogant view of their own strength and no awareness of their impact on others, those who see themselves as God's gift to the human race, may need a strong dose of prophetic censure. They may need the law more than the good news of an appreciative inquiry (though if they participated in a broad-based inquiry, it might show them, surprisingly, how God has been at work in those whom, up till now, they despised).

But in contexts that are challenging, it is not always wise to spend a lot of time examining the problems. I know exactly what is wrong with my sprinkler system at home; I just can't fix it. In the same way, one can become an expert on diagnosing the intricacies of sinful influences but be no closer to building a healthier community. I know for myself that if I were fully aware of all the myriad ways in which my consumer lifestyle, personal actions, and political decisions negatively affect the world around me, I would despair. The truth is, as the doctrine of original sin expresses, I can't escape from contributing to the problems. I can't always know when child labor has been used to cobble a pair of shoes I'm interested in buying. I can't find out the origins of every chocolate bar or banana I eat (though I've made some serious efforts). I can't foresee or prevent all the hurtful outcomes of my actions. I haven't kicked all my bad habits (in fact, I've gained a few!). And I'm closely integrated into the Canadian economy, so I share responsibility for all the ways in which our economy exploits (or is twisted by) its commerce with other countries.

Too much problem-focused diagnosis can degenerate into blame and shame. It can break relationships. It makes us experts on what sin, death, and the devil are up to. But it doesn't bring us any closer to the work that *God* is doing and intends to do in the world. Appreciative inquiry used in a Christian context looks for evidence of the Spirit's movement among us. It tries to teach us how to recognize God at work, to celebrate and get on board with God's community-building mission. More than that, in the very act of sharing stories and dreams, of planning together, that Trinity-shaped community flickers into visible form. Doing appreciative inquiry *is* an experience of trinitarian community.

The impotence of overdiagnosing problems is expressed by Paul in Romans 7. He looks deeply into himself and is thrown into despair: "For I do not do the good I want, but the evil I do not want is what I do. . . . Wretched man that I am! Who will rescue me from this body of death?" (vv. 19, 24). Ironically, looking too deeply at what we've done wrong, or failed to do right, keeps us focused on ourselves. And being curved in on ourselves is, for Luther, the definition of sin. When we constantly worry about our own goodness, or lack of it, when we fret about how God or others will react to our sin, we are still operating in a selfish, self-centered mode. We just want to save our own skin. So we are, in fact, intensifying the underlying problem.

But when we believe God's promise that God will look after our righteousness (that is, our right relationships), we can release that worry. We are free to pay attention to our neighbor. We are free to look closely at what God is up to.

Interestingly, in the well-known chapter on spiritual warfare in Ephesians 6, the armor that Christians are asked to don is almost entirely protective. The battle is not about destroying evil, but about "*standing against* the wiles of the Devil" (v. 11), withstanding, standing firm, quenching "the flaming arrows of the evil one" (vv. 13–16). We are advised to "put on the breastplate of righteousness" (trust God's grace?), "proclaim the gospel of peace," put on "the belt of truth" and "the helmet of salvation" (vv. 14–17). The only offensive weapon is the "word of God," and that is to be wielded by the Spirit (v. 17). We are called to deal with the problems of the world by discerning, proclaiming, trusting in the word and action of *God*. Knowing *God*, not every dark deed of the devil, is the key to new life. A similar theme comes through in Advent texts that admonish us to "Watch" and "Keep awake!" Watch for what? Not to map out every nuance of the Dark One's endeavors but to spot the coming of the *Lord* into our lives and communities.

An *appreciative inquiry* done in a faith context takes for granted the brokenness of human life. But it doesn't let itself get mired in that muskeg. It opens us to the gracious, unexpected action of God in our midst. It allows us to keep God's work on behalf of our neighbor at the center of our attention, directing our action.

I will add one practical caveat however. For appreciative inquiry to be effective in a community, the sufferings of that place must be jointly shared and *publicly* recognized. If there has been open dialogue and formal *lament*, then problems are more likely to be seen as a community responsibility, not simply a private burden.

Lament, it should be noted, is not blame. It is a *communal complaint*: "Something's wrong, God. We are hurting; people we care about are hurting." It brings suffering out into the open so that sufferers can be affirmed (rather than shamed or secluded) and issues can be addressed together.

When some form of common lament has not been voiced, when suffering is silenced by shame or shrouded in denial, the community may not allow an appreciative inquiry to get close to its deepest concerns. In that case, appreciative inquiry may serve simply as a diversion rather than a real investigation into possible futures for those people. It would be as if the early church had been so embarrassed by the manner of Jesus's death that they spent all their time discussing how God may have been at work in Jesus's miracles and missed out on what God was up to in the cross.

However, when a community is able to talk publicly about its core concerns, appreciative inquiry helps hope to grow. It fosters the awareness that God has been at work in this area and that underneath all the suffering, something good has happened—and can happen again.

A Native friend pointed out to me that there is a significant difference in tone between Native newspapers and non-Native newspapers in his city. He said the Native journalists—and their readers—already know in graphic detail the problems their community is dealing with. The laments have already been made, and they don't need more scandals or horror stories to sell their papers. So instead, Native journalists fill the papers with articles of appreciative inquiry: what's working, how young Native people have found meaningful lives, how their community is contributing effectively to our nation's well-being. Not explicitly perhaps, but implicitly, their eyes are focused on the One who makes all things new. Even in the Truth and Reconciliation Commission hearings I attended in Saskatoon where First Nations people told the horrible stories of residential school abuse, I was struck so often by the courage and hope they expressed. Surrounded by family and compassionate friends, their laments—so necessary for our wider Canadian public to hear—were infused with a conviction that our native people have not been abandoned by God.

How to Do an Appreciative Inquiry

There really isn't a single method for appreciative inquiry. In part that is because appreciative inquiry is primarily a perspective and only secondarily a tool or process. Rob Voyle's Clergy Leadership Institute (referred to earlier), which focuses on coaching individuals and leading churches, prefers to speak of "following the appreciative way." The institute offers resources and training opportunities for a variety of ways in which the appreciative perspective can be applied.

Positive questions that focus on what has worked can be used in many different settings. I have used them to help couples in conflict to remember why they love each other and rediscover the gifts in their relationship. The couple's past successes show a path for dealing with the difficult pieces. I've helped discouraged students find new hope by using a green pen to highlight solid work instead of always using a red one and focusing on mistakes. I've helped new ministries use these questions to assess progress toward their goals. And I've found them invaluable as an energy-raising way to enter strategic planning in churches, organizations, and communities.

I've used appreciative inquiry as a way to train seminary interns in mission leadership. As part of training, each intern gathers a group of churched and unchurched people and equips them to carry out a community-building project that will be owned and operated by the people, not the intern. In appendix B, "Steps in Doing a Faith-Based Appreciative Inquiry," I've included material much like that which I give to my interns, outlining the process I want them to follow. You may find some of that useful or be able to adapt it to your purposes.

In general, I like the approach that the Anglican Diocese of New Westminster has taken to apply appreciative inquiry to the renewal of congregational mission. They describe appreciative inquiry when it is applied to organizational change as having five steps:[14]

- Define: Choose the focus of the ministry.
- Discover: Appreciate what is.
- Dream: Imagine what might be.
- Design: Determine what should be.
- Deliver: Create what will be.

As I have done appreciative inquiries and watched interns do them, I've noted that sometimes the process can be ineffective if these steps are skewed by actions or attitudes that don't fit the five core assumptions discussed above. Most important is that the process is allowed to be truly open-ended.

I was asked to do a short version of an appreciative inquiry with a community struggling with economic recession. As we shared stories, many interesting and effective strategies from the past emerged in the Discover phase. But in the Dream section, just as folks were beginning to stretch their imaginations, one of the leaders laid out a fully developed plan. She was going to bring a new commodity into the community and use it to spin off a variety of secondary industries. She pressed it hard. Then it became clear to all the participants that the appreciative inquiry was a personal exercise in salesmanship, not community planning. Her economic plan may have been a great idea, but it didn't emerge out of the people's experience or their own dreams, so they didn't buy in. In fact, they may have felt somewhat manipulated. In the end, little came of the exercise.

In a related sense, the process must also be fully participatory. The Define step should include input from a spectrum broad enough that an issue that really matters to the group in question comes to be the focus. And the Discover stage must include direct input from those involved in various ways in that issue. If youth are the chosen focus but few youth are involved at the Define or Discover stage, any dreams or designs that develop afterward are likely to be wrongheaded and ineffective.

It should be said that a congregation in the Define stage can begin in two ways (though there may be more): they can begin with either a target group or a target area. A target group would be a group of people with a common trait—survivors of sexual assault, empty nesters, young parents, and the like. Or they could begin with a geographic area, such as "a ten-block radius around our church" or "Langdon County" or "the town of Cremona." Either way they would invite people who know a good deal about what goes on in that group or area, and who have various perspectives, to help them focus their interest or concern.

The Discover stage can be done in a variety of formats, such as people interviewing each other one to one, a counselor with a young couple, small groups, and so forth. I have provided a training outline in appendix C, "Doing an Appreciative Inquiry in Small Groups: Guide for Facilitators and Hosts."

The Design stage can be difficult. The large amount of material—story notes, core values, wishes for the future—that emerges from the first three steps must be organized into useful possibilities for action. The people can then choose or modify one of the options presented, create a hybrid, or substitute an option of their own. Cooperrider and Srivastva call these proposals "provocative propositions." They are most likely to capture people's imagination if they draw on the experience of the past but challenge them to move into new areas in new ways. It takes a leadership team with a fair bit of creativity to pull all the experiences, values, and dreams into several doable proposals. I tend to substitute an asset-mapping exercise for this stage because it is less reliant on the skills of a few, increases ownership, and keeps everyone involved, even in the design process.

Finally, the Deliver stage needs clear timelines and specific, realistic objectives. Before the community disperses at the Design stage, they must have an action team in place, a date for a first meeting, and a deadline for reporting back the details. Otherwise, in my experience, the plan can get submerged in the busyness of people's ordinary lives and never happen.

Four More Tips for a Successful Appreciative Inquiry

My first tip is *know thoroughly the key elements of the tool* and *why* they are essential. This allows you to explain it effectively to councils and project members. Don't leave critical elements out. And tying the tool clearly into the core assumptions of their faith helps participants see that the tool fits the nature of the project. The means by which we carry out ministry should be of the same nature as the goals we seek in those ministries. One appreciative inquiry I was involved in was looking for methods that worked in building community spirit. We anticipated that hospitality—food events, especially—would show up as important cohesion builders. So we decided to incorporate a food experience into all of our appreciative inquiry planning sessions and interviews. Besides increasing the joy in the planning, it built in our group the kind of spirit we hoped to discover in the community and gave a deeper integrity to the project.

Second, *practice the tool on a small scale* (for example with the project committee) before engaging in the whole project. This helps to iron out wrinkles and give the committee a full understanding of how the tool works. I cochaired an appreciative research project on how people not connected to churches or formal faith communities nurture their spirituality. In the process of doing a pilot focus group, we discovered that some of the language in our questions (like the term *spirituality*) was a stumbling block to participants. The trial run allowed us to make important adjustments.

Third, *focus on actively equipping congregational or agency or community members* to do the work at *every* stage. Ephesians 4:12

says that pastors are called to "equip the saints for the work of ministry." If an appreciative inquiry is going to actually result in growth or change, it will have to be owned at every stage by the people themselves. The leaders' role is to stand *beside* them, training and resourcing them, rather than in front pulling or pushing from behind.

Fully involving laypeople at every stage in the theory and practice of appreciative inquiry also enables them to incorporate the tool into the nonchurch portion of their lives. They learn to ask, What's working in my marriage? What do I really value about my colleagues and my work? How can I help our dysfunctional staff see the resources and gifts they have in each other and mobilize them? In this way its benefits are spread much more deeply into the community than a single appreciative inquiry might suggest.

Fourth, *generate small, doable action steps.* People can get overwhelmed with large projects and big issues. So it is essential to handle the Deliver section of an appreciative inquiry well. Congregations can get past ideas into real action when they focus on some small, positive thing that *can* be done successfully. The very act of doing it generates new hope, energy, and a sense of satisfaction and self-esteem that fuels future action.

Ultimately, appreciative inquiry is a process of repentance. "Repentance" is a common English translation of the biblical Greek *metanoia,* which means "to change one's mind," "to think differently." When we turn our focus away from ourselves and our world's failures and look for the work of God among us, our lives, and those of our congregations and communities, may be transformed.

CHAPTER 4

Asset Mapping

Doing Mission Like MacGyver

In the last chapter I said that the key to building healthier communities is perspective—seeing the world differently. Asset mapping is an exercise in stewardship that requires, and fosters, a change in perspective.

Key to that change is opening our focus. As Martin Luther was fond of pointing out, "We are not God." That means we are not omniscient, we can't see everything. In fact, our brains are wired to filter out large amounts of information in our environment so that we can focus on, and react quickly to, that which is most important for our survival. Now focus is a good thing. It helped our ancestors keep the saber-toothed tiger in view and not get distracted by ripe fruit. It helps Ph.D. students get their dissertations written sometime before they die. But focus is easily distorted by habit, social conditioning, hormones that react to and reinforce fear, and other factors that can focus our attention too dramatically or keep it constantly trained on just a single part of our environment. We develop "inattentional blindness."[1]

INATTENTIONAL BLINDNESS

Inattentional blindness, a kind of static tunnel vision, keeps us in the church from seeing that (1) *God is at work* in everyone, everywhere, all the time (the previous chapter explored how to remedy one aspect of that vision problem with appreciative inquiry), and

(2) *God has immersed us in gifts* that can be used for building life
and community. The latter is what I will try to address as I explore
asset mapping in this chapter.

A well-known demonstration of inattentional blindness was
carried out by Daniel Simons of the University of Illinois at
Urbana-Champaign and Christopher Chabris of Harvard University. If you would like to conduct a similar demonstration, look
for "moonwalking bear" on YouTube and follow the instructions
before you read the next paragraph.[2]

In the demonstration, Simons and Chabris instructed an audience to watch a video in which three people were wearing white
shirts and three black shirts. He asked them to count how many
times the three in white shirts passed a basketball ball to each other (or other variations on the passes). Afterward, they were asked
if they saw anything unusual. Most said no. When the video was
replayed again, with no instructions as to what to look for, the audience was astonished to see either a woman with an umbrella or
a woman in a gorilla costume walking through the middle of the
group of basketball players. Even though these strange characters
were in the middle of their visual field, very few in the audience
noticed, because they had filtered it out as irrelevant to the ball-
passing count.

Having a wide visual field is essential if one is to be a good steward of God's resources. A steward must be able to see and account
for *all* the resources the owner has supplied—and then mobilize
those resources for the task the steward has been given. But imagine that a grocery store supervisor has been asked by management
to do a store inventory. He ignores the aisles that have fruit in
them because he doesn't like fruit. All the stuff on high shelves is
bypassed because it's too hard to count. Same with the loose vegetables. In fact, this steward ignores virtually every product in the
store, recording just three things: the number of employees and
the cost of their salaries, the size of and furnishings in the building, and the money in the cash registers. Would management be
pleased? Not likely.

Yet, too often that is how churches and their denominational
structures exercise Christian stewardship—carefully tracking

amounts of money, numbers of people (clergy and lay), and the cost of church buildings. But they pay little systematic attention to anything else. When any of these three resources wanes, a congregation's *viability* is questioned. We start to speak of them as *dying*. Eventually we *close* them, not because all the Christians have left or because they have exhausted the work God has given them to do there, but because, in our mind, they are bereft of the resources needed to carry out any significant mission. Operationally, we seem convinced that "the church's one foundation" is *not* "Jesus Christ our Lord" but is a building, a pastor, and a people to pay for them.

Let me suggest that Christian stewardship ought to begin with this theological assertion: *When God wants something done, God provides the resources.* Paul affirms, "God is able to provide you with every blessing in abundance, so that by always having enough of everything, you may share abundantly in every good work" (2 Cor. 9:8). If God invites us into the divine mission, there will be enough to carry it out.

If this is true, why is there such a disconnect between that faith statement and our ecclesiastical perspective? Has God failed to provide for some churches because they have let God down in some way? That is often how congregations with shrinking populations and bank accounts feel. Or is this promise of divine provision an eschatological hope, an ideal that is not necessarily realized in the present? I don't think so. In my experience, the problem is more prosaic: God *has* provided, but we just can't see it.

OPENING OUR FOCUS:
SEEING WITH MACGYVER'S EYES

To understand how this is so, it may help to look at a secular steward. Some readers may remember the character MacGyver from the 1980s TV show by the same name. MacGyver looked at the world around him as a vast collection of possibilities and solutions. Every week he was assigned a mission that turned out to be (apparently) impossible. Unlike James Bond, he wasn't equipped with lasers and flamethrowers, the latest, most expensive technical wizardry. He carried only a Swiss army knife and duct tape. But he did have the most valuable tool that mission agents can have—a set of eyes that could see hidden possibilities. To him the world was full of problem-solving tools. Every broken shoelace, paper clip, bottle cap, piece of pocket lint, and old car battery was potentially part of a conundrum-cracking contraption. Over various episodes, MacGyver took a watch crystal, a map light lens, and a rolled-up newspaper to make a telescope; he used a cell-phone ring and a comb to simulate a police siren; he employed a shoelace and a wrench to put a car on autopilot; he fixed a car radiator by cracking an egg into it; and much more. Faced with certain death each week, MacGyver would creatively mobilize the stuff around him so that he could survive and carry out his assignment.

This ability to see the world as a treasure chest of Tinkertoys, to see endless possibilities in the chaos of its bits and pieces, is not unique to MacGyver. It is one of God's greatest gifts to every human being. Children use it all the time. They lie on their backs on a summer day and pick out castles in the clouds. They scatter Lego blocks on the floor and idly click them together until something interesting begins to form. Psychologists who use drawing or Rorschach images in their diagnosis are relying on this same human ability. Sculptors will often say that they don't know exactly what they are going to carve until they have a block of wood or stone in front of them. They may have a general subject in mind, but it is not until they turn the material over, examine its veins and fissures, its color and textures that a particular image emerges.

One of our emeritus professors tells about a time when a great artist came to speak at our seminary's spring conference. The artist told the assembly that if one has eyes to see, there is beauty in everything. Afterward a fellow came up to him with a piece of paper in his hand. He said, "You claim there is beauty in everything. Well, I love what my two-year-old daughter draws because I love *her.* But look at what she was doing while you were talking. You can't tell me there's real beauty in that." He showed the artist the paper covered with the toddler's scratches and wobbly lines. The artist examined it for a moment, turned it around several times, and finally said, "Ah, yes, I see it now, right in the center—a pony." And then he pointed out certain marks—and suddenly the father could see it too—the rough, broken outline of a pony. Was that the child's creative skill at work? Probably not. Rather it was the artist's creative *eye*—the ability to see what others cannot—to find the possibilities hidden in that rude jumble of squiggly lines.

ASSET MAPPING AS
SEEING THE REAL—NOT THE IDEAL

In the King James version of the Bible, Proverbs 29:18 is translated, "Where there is no vision, the people perish." This is true (though the translation is flawed). The real poverty of communities in crisis is not the loss of jobs or local institutions or young people—bad as those are. Nor is it bankruptcy, hunger, or even homelessness. It's the loss of hope. It's the paralyzing blindness that creeps over a people, preventing them from seeing and mobilizing the amazing resources hidden among them.

Exactly what *kind* of vision do such people need? There is Plato's sort of vision—the perfect ideal, which is apprehended inwardly and then brought to rough expression in reality. Designers often employ this vision. They imagine a structure, design it on paper, and then go out to find a company that can bring in the necessary materials and labor to build it.

Then there is MacGyver's sort of vision. It begins with the real rather than the ideal. And it is not primarily interested in *need*— the dark holes in life. MacGyver focuses not on what he wants or once had or feels he should have, but on that which is *actually there* in the space around him. His vision filters out nothing, initially treating *everything*—materials, skills, relationships, access— as potentially useful in the right combinations. He sees connections and patterns among disparate elements, some of which turn out to be wonderfully useful for his immediate situation.

This is the vision that asset mapping encourages. We begin with *what is*, not what isn't. Asset mapping helps us see possibilities deep in this present reality and, like the sculptor, seeks to coax those possibilities out of it, removing obstacles in order to aid their emergence. Then we pray that God will breathe life into what has been discovered.

Note that asset mapping is more than simply noticing or even cataloguing resources. Cataloguing is what time and talent surveys do. Too often, those lists languish on office shelves or in computer files, rarely consulted. And they often leave those who filled out the sheets feeling insulted that they weren't taken up on the offer of their gifts.

In addition, time and talent surveys tend to rely on the vision of a single leader to identify where and how the catalogued gifts might be employed. Here is where the MacGyver metaphor could be misinterpreted. For the key in asset mapping as we do it is not to find a single MacGyver who alone sees and connects the gifts of the whole community, but to help the community *as a whole* to see and act like MacGyver. So in the form of asset mapping described in this chapter, the people themselves identify their gifts but also go on to *connect* and *mobilize* them in community action. There is broad investment not only in the gifts but also in the *process* by which they are mobilized, and as a result, there is true ownership of the product or project that emerges.

Asset mapping gains its power by enlisting a congregation or community to play with the mapped resources in such a way that they can see patterns and connect varied resources to create many new forms of effective ministry. One of the problems with the human capacity for creative pattern recognition is that we can discern patterns on the basis of very little input, as group facilitators Jon and Maureen Jenkins point out.[3] They mention the example of two lights gradually getting larger and farther apart. We interpret that as an approaching car. But the lights could signify other things (two motorcycles?). For this pattern-recognition capacity to work in our favor as we plan ministry, we must be willing to look at as much available data as possible and to suspend judgment for a time so that the creative process isn't cut short—not assuming that the first solution, or the one we have been trained to recognize, is necessarily the best.

I am indebted to Luther Snow, who has developed extensive tools for asset-mapping in congregations and communities.[4] Further on I will describe one process that I have used with students and congregations but it is best to consult the resources of Snow and others to see the wide variety of ways one can do and apply asset-mapping.[5] The process I will describe involves bringing a group of congregation or community members together around a common interest (such as seniors). The group is divided into subgroups of five, each at their own table. Each person has a set of cards on which they write, in response to the leader's questions, things that they do for fun, things they'd be willing to lend, people who owe them a favor, institutions and natural resources to which they have access, and so forth. Everyone's cards are then laid out on the table, and the group tries to connect these various resources to create a new form of ministry in their area of interest.

So, for example, when one of my students led an asset-mapping exercise, his congregation discovered that in their large town a lot of seniors had extra space in their homes and wanted someone to live with them. Having a housemate made the seniors feel secure, because their health was frail or unpredictable. At the same time, the community had an influx of young, mostly single, oil industry-related workers who couldn't find housing. In response, a group from the congregation and community developed a Home Share program that matched (and screened) seniors who had rooms with newcomers who needed housing and had companionship and home maintenance skills to offer. The program was so successful that the provincial government picked it up.

Another student did an asset-mapping exercise regarding seniors and youth that found a connection between regional mountain trails, girls' love of pajama parties, and grandparents and grandchildren's mutual appreciation. It resulted in Take a Hike, Gran! in which grandparents and youth went on a half-day hike together on a local trail, and Grannies and Jammies—a pajama party for grandmothers and granddaughters.

Barrier to Seeing the Real: Convergent Thinking

The problem is, congregations often aren't used to exercising this sort of vision in their planning processes. It's not surprising. Community development analyst James Cook claims this is generally true of institutions and community systems. He says community development theory assumes "breadth of experience, intelligence, information and energies represented in a population far exceed that which the community system takes into account."[6]

This is likely due in part to the fact that no system can easily track the enormously diverse and constantly changing set of resources and relationships in a human community. But it may also be that institutions and other community systems restrict their awareness of diversity in order to keep themselves stable. UNC professor of orthopedic medicine Frank Wilson, for example, points out in his article "No Tempests, No Teapots" that schools train us early on that to be different is to be disruptive or disorderly. He says, "The need for structure and discipline encourages convergent rather than divergent behavior." For Wilson it is divergent, "out of the box" thinking that defines creativity. Creativity for him is "bringing something new into existence by recognizing a relationship between previously unassociated elements. . . . Human creation results not ex nihilo but from the *use of existing material in unusual ways*."[7]

As institutions, churches may also encourage convergent thinking. From childhood they teach us the importance of right—or ideal—beliefs. We are trained to conform to a common ideal by reciting creeds, memorizing uniform catechisms, participating in common liturgies, or adhering to ethical norms. Doubt is often treated with suspicion—as a sign of unfaithfulness or heresy—even though people of deep faith know that doubt is faith's essential companion. Doubt draws attention to divergent elements in the world that one's present faith cannot account for and prompts faith to stretch to embrace them.

It is also easy for congregations to become captive to a static ideal of church. Many watch the megachurch broadcasts on TV that tell them what the church really ought to be. Usually, it ought to be a good deal bigger. A truly God-pleasing congregation, it seems, should draw the crowds. This idealistic thinking is often reflected in frequent references to a golden age in a congregation's past when it was bigger and better.

Clergy don't necessarily help in these matters. Depending on their training, they may have had years in seminary sorting out heresy from truth, absorbing images of ideal belief, ideal Christian behavior, ideal churches, and ideal pastors. It's not surprising that, in their early years of ministry at least, they frequently seem determined to fashion themselves and their people into that ideal image—at least until the inevitable disillusionment sets in.

Unfortunately, when congregations age and decline, as all do (since no congregations that I am aware of live forever), this sort of idealism leads to shame. Instead of seeing who they are, they can see only who they are not. They are not the bustling young congregation with noisy children in every pew that they once were. They don't have the income to hire a full-time pastor and a youth director as they did in the golden years. There is a sense of having failed God and the ancestors in the faith. A posture of helpless dependency develops as people realize that the ideal will only be achievable with an infusion of outside resources—new people into the community or money from the wider church or a dynamic new pastor. Under that awareness, suggestions for change meet resistance. Many church folks don't really like depending on outside support, and they aren't sure that it will actually materialize; and even if it does, they suspect it won't be there for the long term. They don't believe that dynamic pastors would ever be attracted to their declining church. So, while they yearn for the ideal church, deep down they despair that it isn't realizable.

LEARNING TO COUNT *ALL* THE GIFTS

When I work with struggling congregations, I offer them a different way of viewing ministry. For example, I invited one group of rural church leaders to imagine that overnight, across denominations, God killed all the clergy, struck every church with lightning and burnt them all to the ground, then evaporated the bank accounts of every congregation. They were left with no money, no clergy, no buildings (the components normally understood to be essential to a viable congregation), just a smoking pile of ash in the center of their town and a funeral to attend.

After giving the participants a moment to mourn, we did an asset-mapping exercise. First, I asked them to name, from their own context, what they had left to do ministry with. They were stumped at first. But slowly, as they began to turn their eyes away from the trinity that normally occupies their attention (money, clergy, and buildings), a list began to develop that was surprisingly long. It included natural resources (rivers, parks, caves, lakes, forests, and so on), people's skills, things they were willing to give or lend, time, spiritual experience and biblical knowledge, local institutions (such as hospitals and schools), and programs (such as wood carving). It included businesses, personality characteristics, community members with leadership ability, folks who owed them a favor and might be willing to contribute ("Tom runs the hockey arena and might let us use it for a youth skating party"), and more. Then I asked them, in regional groups, to connect these resources in a way that would allow them to participate effectively in God's mission in their local setting.

At first they wanted to find a way to rebuild the church, recreate what they once had. But I asked them to rule that out. Gradually, as they caught the sense that this was to be something new, the groups came up with wonderful, off-the-wall ideas. One region imagined a partnership with the local hospital, offering a ministry of music, healing touch, prayer, and conversation. Another drafted a plan for a community pig roast, advertised in hair salons and coffee row, to draw the whole community into a discussion about its spiritual well-being. A third imagined partnering with a local coffee shop and bookstore to offer a community kitchen, Eucharist, and weekly explorations of the spirituality of hairdressing, home care, and other community-building roles, treating them as ministries. None of these options was pie-in-the-sky, because they were built out of resources that the participants actually had. And the groups didn't have to be sold on their ideas, because they themselves had created them.

Seeing that they had many options for ministry, participants said that they felt much less anxiety and more energized about their situation. They saw that God's mission could take many effective forms, no matter what the size of their congregation or community. Ironically, without a single new dollar in the offering plate, without one new seat in the pew—in fact, having experienced a catastrophic *loss* of buildings, money, and clergy—they moved in their own minds from being poor to being rich.

The reality is that almost everything around us, and in us, can be used by God for ministry. Yet in the church we have developed the habit of noticing and tabulating only a very few resources. We have treasurers, treasurer's reports, accounting software, annual audits, reports to national church structures, and a host of other mechanisms for keeping track of monetary resources. We have custodians, altar guilds, deacons, property committees, insurance agents, building audits, and annual reports to track and care for our church structures. And we have seminaries, national rosters, bishops or supervisors, clergy conferences, and clergy compensation and support structures to train, care for, and keep track of our professional ministers. But which churches pay that kind of deliberate attention to the skills and personalities of their people or to the natural resources around them or to their potential partners in the community? Which churches tabulate and celebrate them? Which churches contemplate them long enough to see fruitful connections for new ministries? Only those that learn to see ministry through MacGyveresque eyes.

ASSET MAPPING AS BRICOLAGE

The French call people like MacGyver "bricoleurs." While it may not be often encouraged in the church's stewardship, bricolage is a common practice in the stewardship of everyday life. For example, I have several musicians in my family. They creatively stitch together a living by keeping an eye out for gigs, teaching opportunities, any chance to share their music. The farmers I know tend to be bricoleurs, especially at harvest time. When the clouds are threatening rain and the combine breaks down, they can create remarkable solutions out of binder twine, chicken wire, and old combine parts. And farm women have a history of taking fabric scraps in wildly different colors and shapes to sew into beautifully patterned quilts. Of course, all of us engage in bricolage when we enter the kitchen to make a meal out of what we find in the fridge. A transformation, an alchemy occurs as flour, spices, eggs, fruit, vegetables, meat, and milk are brought together with heat to make food that is new and nourishing. Bricoleurs are creative, self-reliant people who look at the world as a treasure chest of resources. They are determined to make gold out of the various bits of lead lying around in their lives.

It is heartening to me that people view many issues in their noninstitutional lives through the lens of a bricoleur. It means that when they come to church, that set of lenses, though it may not be resting on their noses, is still available in their purse or breast pocket. The key is to help them take out those glasses and use them to look at ministry in a new way. And the Bible can help with that.

GOD AND CREATION:
INVENTING COMMUNITY TOGETHER

In chapter 1 we looked at the sociality of God—the idea that God is not a lonely monarch but is a rich, dynamic community that acts as one because each person takes the others into account.

While we can't really examine the inner life of God in any detail, the stories of God's people allow us to see something of how God acts in the world (the "economic" Trinity). And God's action appears to be very much like that of a bricoleur—of one who takes *everything* into account ("even the hairs of your head are all counted" [Matt. 10:30]). In relating to creation, Israel, and the church, God is constantly portrayed as adaptive, inventing. God makes plans and revises them, initiates relationship and then adjusts to our response. God mobilizes the most unusual and even despised resources. The biblical picture of God is not that of an engineer who designs a universe, builds it to perfect standards, sets it in motion (like a watchmaker), and then shows up only for routine maintenance.

Rather, God works with what's there, with the chaos in Genesis 1:1 and the chaos from Genesis 1:27 on, when human beings enter the picture. What's *there* is often not at all what God might have thought is ideal. Yet God adapts in a way that brings marvelous new things into being. Early on humans mess things up. Yet their sin sets the stage for God to offer the greatest expression of love in Christ. Moses is a murderer—but God sees that he is the right man in the right place to challenge Pharaoh for Israel's freedom. And

Pharaoh is stubborn as a mule—but God uses that stubbornness to create opportunities to demonstrate God's power and faithfulness to Israel and to Egypt. God adjusts to Abraham's fears, Jacob's schemes, David's lust, Delilah's betrayal, Judas's sellout of his Lord. And Jesus assembles the most motley crew of disciples one can imagine, yet the Spirit finds a way to bring to the world a glimpse of the new creation through them. From the random stuff of these characters' lives—the good, the bad, and the ugly—God finds a way to foster life. Paul says it in Romans 8:28: "In everything God works for good."

This same bricolage seems to characterize not only God's behavior but also ours (that is, all of creation's). In the first chapter I noted that the universe, as we currently understand it, is composed of relationships in constant, dynamic adaptation. So we should not imagine creation as a machine running on fixed, absolute principles, as Newton was pushed to assert. Rather, space, time, matter, and energy all interact in a complex and constantly changing web of relationships.[8] Even time changes as one entity moves relative to another.

The Bible supports that picture. Its portrayal of creation challenges any idea that the universe is mechanical—a collection of dead atoms. Biblical writers are convinced that creation shares in the life of God. John 1 tells us that "all things came into being through him [the Son]" and that "what has come into being in him is *life*," like God (italics mine). Job 38:29 asks, "From whose womb did the ice come forth, and who has given birth to the hoarfrost of heaven?" Colossians 1 speaks of Christ as the "firstborn of all creation," the one "*in* whom," "*through* whom," and "*for* whom" all things were created and hold together. It is not so surprising, then, that Genesis 1:27 can insist that even we human creatures— often ungodly, it seems—bear the imprint of God's image. From passages like these, the ancient church came to believe that the universe finds its source in the Father, its pattern in the Son, its life in the Spirit.

So—if *God* is creative and the universe bears the spittin' (that is, spirit and) image of the Creator, it is no surprise to find that the Bible describes God's *world* as being inventive too. Look at

Genesis 1:11, 20, and 24. God says, "Let the *earth* bring forth . . . ,"
"Let the *waters* bring forth . . . ," as if the land and sea were given a
generative task (italics mine).

This is not to suggest that creatures can bring forth things out
of *nothing,* as God can. But clearly God's creation reflects something of God's own extraordinary creativity. The universe is dynamic, capable of surprises and possibilities. Nor is it to imply that
creation is on its own, *independently* generating its own changes.
Genesis 1 describes a wonderful interaction between *God's* making (for example, the sea monsters) and the *earth's* making (for
example, "bringing forth" plants and animals). God is not passive in, or absent from, creation. Rather, God is actively present
everywhere, around and in every grain of sand, Luther says. God
is intimately involved with creation's ongoing growth but in a way
that includes human and nonhuman creativity. So Adam (earth-
ling) comes into being out of both the earth's and God's action.
And Adam provides finishing touches to the joint creative activity
by naming various creatures.

This interaction between God and creation is characterized
by three things. First, on God's part, it is characterized by love.
God's omnipresence, the permeation of all creation by the Spirit,
is not designed primarily to *invade* or *control.* Rather the Bible
insists that God is everywhere present in order to *love* creation intimately. After all, God *is* love—a community of persons in deeply
loving, freely responding relationship. So it makes sense that God
would want that sort of relationship in and with creation.

We see that all-embracing love expressed in Genesis 9:8–17.
After the flood, God makes a covenant—a promise of love—that
is repeated several times. With whom is the covenant made? Four
times humans are included, but *six* times *all* living creatures are
mentioned, and at least once the whole earth is the object of the
promise. Clearly God wants, and has, a living, loving relationship
with *all* creation. And the Bible assumes the potential for a responsive love *from* creation. Psalm 98:8 (and many other passages) speak about the floods, the trees, stones, animals responding
to God in praise.

Second, that love relationship requires and safeguards *freedom.* There is freedom for God to say no to our prayers, for example. And there is freedom for creatures to act and respond as they will; otherwise, they would be simply God's machines. We know this to be true not only of thinking animals but even at the atomic level. For example, it has long been known that radioactive atoms decay into their stable isotopes in an unpredictable way. One atom may decay after five minutes. A neighboring atom of the same radioactive element may wait one hundred years or one thousand. Atoms seem to have some freedom in the matter!

Finally, creation's freedom comes at a price. It means that some of the things that galaxies, the earth, and we humans come up with in our freedom are poorly adapted, short-lived experiments. Too often they are evil. As a result, the long history of our becoming has invariably been marked with struggle, suffering, and even disaster.

In giving us this freedom to fail, we see the humility of God's love. In creation God self-limits. So God does not do all the making but shares generative power with us; we are told and enabled to "be fruitful and multiply." God not only speaks but also listens as we pray. God is not the only one whose will is done; our will is done too (though the Bible tells of God's anger and sorrow when it is far different from God's own; see for example Gen. 6:6).[9]

The divine humility is most deeply—and mysteriously— expressed in Christ's incarnation. For in the cross of Jesus, God endures creation's darkest deed, insisting that even that most violent of our choices shall not separate us from God's love. And Easter morning reveals the true extent of God's creative freedom, as God brings into being, out of this travesty of death and betrayal, a *new* creation in Christ.

Seeing this amazing history of divine bricolage allows me to look back on our human history with faith. I can believe that in the biblical flood, in the meteorite that wiped out the dinosaurs, in the painful struggles of my own life, and even in death (and our planet has seen *lots* of it), God is present, working with what is there, working with what we've done for good or ill, to bring new life.

As I noted in the previous chapter, God stands not only behind and with us but also ahead of us, in our future, *drawing* this world through all its decisions and struggles toward the new creation, yet without forcing it. Paul expresses this idea in 1 Corinthians 15:13 when he says, "If there is no resurrection of the dead, then Christ has not been raised." He repeats it in verse 16, "For if the dead are not raised, then Christ has not been raised." The implication is that the cause of Christ's resurrection is not in the past (where we usually assume causes to be) but in the future. The resurrection of the dead at the end of time has reached back to draw forth this first, deep expression of risen life in the person of Jesus Christ.

Interestingly, some scientific, experimental evidence indicates that the universe works this way—that it is influenced not only by the past but apparently also by the *future*. In 2008 an experiment at the University of Rochester showed that the deflection of laser light was affected by events that *followed* the deflection. It turns out that in these experiments the future may be affecting the past—not in a determinative, controlling way in each instance. But it can be seen as an overall pattern when one looks at many repetitions of the experiment.[10]

To think of God working in this way, one might imagine God as a jazz conductor, standing ahead of us, encouraging creatures to freely create their own riffs on the divine melodies but directing us back to the core tune when we get too far off-key or fail to listen to our neighbors in the band.

Building Resilience in Congregations and Communities

Of course, to say that God stands ahead of us drawing us into the future is not to say that that future is foreordained, even less that it unfolds in a predictable straight line. The first decade of the twenty-first century has taught us that. Things change—often suddenly and unexpectedly: September 11, the wars in Afghanistan and Iraq, Hurricane Katrina, the 2006 tsunami, the world's economic meltdown in 2008, and 2010's devastating earthquakes. Trends—economic, political, or otherwise—don't last long.

Rural communities understand this fairly well. For the most part, they rely on resource-based economies, which can be notoriously capricious. The copper ore runs out and a mine closes, putting half the town out of work. The market value of potash or grain hits the stratosphere one year and crashes the next. A new oil deposit is discovered, and overnight dozens of oil workers are moved in, putting enormous stress on a town's facilities.

To live well under these changing conditions requires resilience. Congregations that develop the eyes of MacGyver, the habits of a bricoleur, are well situated to contribute to their communities' resilience. They become faithful stewards of community resources, continually noticing and creatively mobilizing them in ways that allow the community to successfully adapt to the unexpected.

In fact, congregations can bring some peculiarly important gifts to community resilience. A three-year study by the University of Queensland looked for elements that contribute to resilience in rural communities.[11] One of those elements is a strong belief system. Among its findings, the study noted the following contributions that churches make to community resilience:

First, churches help foster a sense that all are connected and called to serve one another. That belief increases the likelihood that residents will volunteer their time for activities that support community life.

Second, churches offer rituals that help communities process change. Subjects in the study spoke about the importance of coming-of-age rituals for young people that help them sort out who they are and how the values of their childhood might connect with who they are becoming. Without the church's rituals, young people tended to see coming of age as getting a driver's license or getting drunk for the first time (often fatally combining the driving and the drinking). Church rituals also help a community to grieve—to lament the loss of a beloved member or to implore God for help when unemployment steals their hope. And rituals help a community to celebrate its milestones together, to remember its history and to see God at work, especially in its struggles. Who will lead these rituals if not those who have been trained in the liturgies of life?

Third, churches help a community to hope by providing a sense of coherence or meaning to their common life. When change disrupts the rhythms of a people, it can be easy to feel that life is chaotic. If nothing is predictable, then trying to rebuild is futile. But if under all the uncertainty there rests a divine steadfastness that is more solid than the forces that rip us apart, it is possible to imagine that we could try again successfully. If nothing is tried, then entropy and chaos increase, and there is even less energy to try something new. But with hope, one can experiment. Not every effort will be successful, but some things will work, perhaps better than before. New energy is released and the community is better able to adapt to whatever its future brings.

It should also be noted, however, that the Queensland study found that congregational exclusivism (denominations protecting their turf against each other, congregations spending time worrying about who is in, who is out) worked against resilience. It harmed the community's capacity to work effectively together to deal with new challenges. Ecumenical and interfaith cooperation conversely had a positive effect.

Fourth, churches can help a community see a wider spectrum of wealth. Governments and economic entities tend to look at the world with slitted glasses, which allow resources to been seen only in a narrow band consisting of money, commodities, and educated people. But churches—though they also succumb to this thinking—have in their traditions an awareness that every community is surrounded and infused by the Spirit of God. The Spirit energizes every child, every blade of grass, every relationship and memory and makes it possible for them *all* to contribute to the community's well-being. This awareness is the particular genius of asset mapping.

How Does One Do Asset Mapping?

As mentioned earlier, I like the approach to asset mapping that Luther Snow uses in *The Power of Asset Mapping: How Your*

Congregation Can Act on Its Gifts (Alban, 2004) and on his website (www.luthersnow.com). Unlike many asset-mapping resources, Snow goes beyond simply *mapping* (that is, keeping track of or cataloguing) assets to *mobilizing* them in creative ways. He makes use of the self-organizing principle so often found in nature, which I mentioned in chapter 1. Rather than imposing an idea generated by a single visionary leader, this process generates ideas by putting people and resources into tight interaction with each other. As people are helped to take notice of each other and their resources, to look for ways to connect them, like putting together the pieces of a jigsaw puzzle, pictures of new ministries gradually emerge.

Other resources you may find helpful are

- *Asset-Based Strategies for Faith Communities* by Susan Rans and Hilary Altman (Chicago: Institute for Policy Research, Northwestern University, 2002). Good stories.
- The Asset-Based Community Development Institute, www.abcdinstitute.org. Helpful ways of cataloguing assets.

Supplies

Gather the following supplies to use in the asset-mapping process:

- Three-by-five-inch cards (or large Post-it notes), five or six per person
- Felt-tip writing markers (one per person)
- Tables
- Newsprint and stand, or blackboard
- Sticky dots (at least three per person)—*optional*
- Tape or poster putty for hanging newsprint on walls

Presentation of Situation, Area of Concern, or Interest

Before beginning to map assets for the first time I have found it helpful to identify a focus for the exercise. The focus may be given by the group's own purpose (a congregational youth committee for example). It may grow out of strategic planning or an appreciative inquiry ("we've decided we want to enhance the hospitality in our community"). Sometimes a large donor specifies a general area in which they would like to support new ministry. A community need or tragedy (flooding, school shooting, toxic train derailment, mine closure) may provoke the desire to develop a creative response. Interest may be generated by the discovery of a hidden population (shut-in elderly, chil-dren with intellectual disabilities, new immigrants).

Help your group discuss the area of interest without suggesting how to engage it. You want to ensure that they have gathered all the facts they can about what is happening. But they should suspend their judgment about how to respond to those facts. This is sometimes difficult, but essential. The outcome of the exercise must not be pre-determined.

Note that as your experience with and confidence in this process grows, the exercise can also be done without identifying an area of interest—simply allowing options to surface in an open-ended way with no preconceived outcomes. Projects may emerge that address unarticulated community hopes or that support existing programs.

Time Required

The normal time required to do the asset-mapping exercise described below with a group is about two-and-a-half hours. It can be modified for less time. It also benefits from the addition of a fifteen- or twenty-minute refreshment break as part of step 6 so that participants can reflect on the options that have emerged before they vote. Generally ideas are better formed when they aren't rushed.

Steps in the Mapping Assets Process

1. **Divide into groups.** Five or six people per table. Thirty to thirty-five index cards per table plus one felt-tipped pen per person.
2. **Deal the cards.** Each person takes four cards. The rest can remain off to the side of the table and may or may not be used during the mapping process.

3. **Fill out the cards.**
   A. *Initial.* Have each person put their initials in the bottom right corner of each card they use. This allows the gifts and their owners to remain connected during the mapping.
   B. *Instruct.* Explain that participants will *write one response (it can be a word or phrase) per card,* writing fairly large and legibly so that everyone can read the cards from three or four feet away.
   C. *Write.* Depending on the situation or area of interest or concern, choose four of the following directions and invite the group to write down responses on their cards. *They should write down only things they would actually be willing to use, offer, or access in some way.*
      (1) List one thing you like to do or have done several times for fun.
      (2) List one thing your congregation does well.
      (3) List one institution, association, or club in your town to which you are well connected (besides your church).
      (4) List one thing you would be willing to lend or donate if needed.
      (5) List one natural resource in this area to which you have access.
      (6) List one thing people might say you are good at.
      (7) List one person with whom you have a strong connection who
         a. has leadership skills for motivating and organizing people that he or she might be willing to exercise *if you asked.*
         b. has any of the above in (1) to (6) that he or she might be willing to share. Indicate on the card the person's name and what resource you think he or she would share if you asked.
4. **Connect the cards to create a project or ministry.** Have each group spread its cards out on the table. Ask groups to take a few minutes to look at the cards, ask questions of the card writers if the phrases on them are unclear,

and then begin to move the cards around into interesting groupings. Imagine what could be done with these groupings to address the situation or area of interest or concern. After several ideas have surfaced, invite the group to decide which one or two they would be interested in pursuing. The ideas should be fleshed out, with additional resources that the group actually has, if needed.

5. **Present the projects.** Invite each group to write its best idea on a sheet of newsprint. (Be careful when using markers with newsprint, so marker ink doesn't bleed through to the table. Double up the newsprint).

   A. *Hang up newsprint sheets (completed)* on the walls of the gathering space using poster putty or tape (as the wall surface permits).

   B. *Explain each group's idea* to the larger assembly. Ask one person from each group to present the idea. At the end of each presentation, the facilitator asks if other members from that group have anything to add, and then asks if anyone in the general assembly has any questions.

   C. *Consolidate.* If two or more presentations are very similar, hang them together as a single project concept.

6. **Choose.** Have the whole assembly vote on the ideas that come out of the groups. Give each person three sticky dots for voting. People should walk around, read the sheets, and place their dots. They can place all three dots on one idea or split them up. This is often a good place in the process for a refreshment break, which gives people time to reflect.

7. **Organize for action.**

   A. *Select an action committee* to get the project underway. Identify volunteers from the assembly who might be willing to contribute to the most popular plan. Write down their names. Since those who came up with the ideas did so out of resources they themselves wrote down and are willing to use, the leader should expect volunteers from this group but from others as well.

B. *Choose a facilitator and host* for the first meeting. The facilitator will remind others of the meeting times and place and will coordinate the conversation at the first meeting.

C. *Schedule time and place* for the first meeting.

8. **Debrief.** Ask the whole group: What surprised you? What was difficult? In what ways has this exercise changed the way you view your congregation or community?

Tips for the Facilitator

When introducing the project-building step (step 4), tell the groups:

- *Expect an initial period of uncertainty.* It will feel a bit chaotic at first. Be patient with that. Ideas always emerge eventually.
- *Think out loud, even if you tend to be quieter in a group.* Something you say might trigger a thought or connection for someone else.
- *Don't judge the viability of your ideas initially.* Just get several out on the table, even if they initially seem outlandish. It's a brainstorming exercise. You will have time to sort through them after a bit.
- *Don't just group similar assets,* even if there are a number of duplicates among the cards. This is important. The creativity of this exercise comes through connecting *different* resources. For example, if you had someone with carpentry skills, you might put that card together with people who like to write and people who have musical skills, and together you could put on a musical. It is in the *connections* between resources that possibilities appear. Of course, if it turns out that there are a lot of resources in a certain area, that could be interesting too. A lot of folks with carpentry skills might suggest starting a woodworking club for seniors or rehabbing houses for single parents and widows. But even those sorts of projects would

require other skills such as leadership, phoning, connections to seniors or single parents, financial accounting, and so on.

During the project-building step (step 4), circulate among the groups and be prepared to do the following:

- *Inhibit efforts to group similar items.* This is by far the most common tendency of groups and is rarely productive as an initial step. Encourage participants to look for connections between items that are *different*.
- *Watch for a leadership vacuum.* If no one wants to step up and make a suggestion, you might look at the cards yourself, see if there are a couple of interesting connections, and say, "What could we do with [for example] the fishing boat, the senior's lodge, and Joan's teaching skills?" If no one responds, make a tentative suggestion (for example, offering a class in tying flies and a fly-fishing outing for seniors). Indicate that there are many such possibilities. Ask, "Does anyone see some other connections among the cards?" Wait patiently for a response and affirm it.
- *Help groups go deeper.* As ideas emerge ask, "What might be the *impact* if we did something like this in our congregation or community?" "What else would you need to make this happen?" "What resources do you have access to, to meet those needs?" "What sort of challenges might you have to overcome?"
- *Watch for controlling behavior.* Often a group member with high status in the congregation or community, or a strong personality, will push his or her idea hard or critique another's in an aggressive way. Gently but firmly help the group to stay open: "That's a very interesting idea, Chris. What others have emerged?" Or, "Mary, have you noticed any connections that seem interesting to you?"
- *Affirm both intuitive and practical skills.* Some people will be better in the early part of the exercise at noticing

connections and integrating resources. Others will be better, as ideas emerge, at putting legs on the idea and at identifying practical challenges and the need for additional resources.

- *Keep time.* Help groups move along, especially if they get bogged down on small details. Remind them that detailed planning will take place once the whole assembly has decided on a project. Encourage them to get their idea onto the newsprint.
- *Identify a presenter in each group.* As the time approaches for groups to present the ideas they have put on newsprint, make sure that one of the group members has been appointed by the group to present it.
- *Affirm* their creative, out-of-the-box thinking. Most participants will not have done an exercise like this. Give lots of positive feedback: "Interesting!" "Wow!" "That's creative!" and the like.

What Characterizes Successful Asset-Mapping Exercises?

I have found that paying attention to a few basic principles increases the likelihood that asset mapping will be fruitful.

First, those who generate an idea must be the primary leaders for carrying it out. This is true primarily because the resources that were interconnected to generate the idea belong to them. This is not to say that others might not be attracted to an idea and join their efforts. But to be successful, a project must be owned and operated by the people who invent it.

Doreen used asset mapping to generate several out-of-the-box ideas for her church committees. But when those ideas were reviewed by the church council, she reported, "The congregational council is reluctant to move on the ideas generated, because they fear the indicators that they have collected are from too small a congregational sample." The council was assuming that the exercise simply generated ideas that others would have to implement. They worried that the rest of the congregation wouldn't be interested in the ideas or wouldn't have the resources to carry them out. And they were quite right. Just because MacGyver was able to use his bricolage skills to create a telescope out of eyeglasses and a newspaper to deal with his particular need, it wouldn't be appropriate for him to then recommend that hunters, soldiers, and astronomers in need of vision enhancement do the same.

Asset-mapped projects are inherently contextual and rooted in specific people, times, and places. They ought not to be universalized, assuming that others should get on board because "this is the best way to do things." Communities are inherently messy. People behave in one way in one role and in other ways in other roles— and differently at different times in the same role. What works now for this group of folks may not work for them later or for the rest of the congregation or community at any time.

One positive side effect of a "those who dream it, do it" approach is a reduction in the amount of permission seeking that new ministries must undergo. If a group of people wants to make something good happen and they have the resources to do it, a council is less likely to resist. They can see that it may not draw on exhausted congregational funds or volunteers. Kristen said that she wanted to avoid overburdening her congregation with one more thing to be done. So she began her focus group asking, "Let's do something together that will reduce your stress. What is it that stresses you?" The women told her that loneliness was a key stressor, because their men worked away from home for days or weeks at a time. The asset-mapping exercise led to communal cooking groups that brought the women relief from a daily chore and built friendships. The groups became a source of energy and joy, not one more drain on scarce congregational resources.

A second key to success flows from keeping the design, supply, and implementation of a project for the most part within the same group of people: *it keeps projects small.* While a few of our interns' projects have been large and unexpectedly successful (like the Home Share program mentioned above), it is generally not wise to dream big.

Big dreams tend to acquire an engineering or ideal character. The tendency is to treat the project mechanistically—to draw the plan, gather the component parts, and then assemble. But like the rest of creation, churches and communities are organisms, not machines. In an organism, each cell already has the essentials of life but needs to be effectively connected to those beside it. The most adaptive form of those relationships can't be predetermined. So organic growth proceeds one step at a time, like crystals growing from a single molecule or cells reproducing and connecting with nearby neighbors (remember principles of trinitarian community from the first chapter) without having a clear understanding of what the ultimate—if there is an "ultimate"—shape of the organism might be. It's through such small changes that a community evolves, learning to adapt to its environment. But if an organization is committed to a single, large project spread over several years, it is very hard to abandon the project if things suddenly change. Simple inertia, and the desire not to see previous effort wasted, will keep people working at a large undertaking far beyond the point where it is useful.

When a project is small it is also more achievable. The old saw is true, in my experience: success breeds success. Especially in situations where the future seems grim and resources scarce, a failed project, particularly if it is the first effort, can put the kibosh on future projects: "We tried that once: it didn't work!"

Third, be patient. Both appreciative inquiry and asset mapping work against the gravity of church tradition and human nature to some extent. So it takes time and repeated efforts (in different ways) to change the culture and mindset of a congregation. Long-entrenched habits don't disappear overnight. As stated above, working hard at successfully doing something small helps encourage the doing of something bigger. It sets down a track. If the first journey is successful, we are more likely to take that way next time, and eventually a highway may develop. Regarding timelines, be wary of grants from foundations and governments. They are often require very short completion schedules and do not take into account the time needed for people to absorb new ideas and generate new relationships. Rushing a venture to meet granters' deadlines may sabotage the project and sour the idea of further projects in the minds of the community.

A final key to success is to see any project that emerges as a means for building people, rather than the people as resources for carrying out the project. God's project began with the words "Let us make humankind in our image" (Gen. 1:26), not "Let us make human beings *do . . .*" If the mission of God is to build a community that reflects the life of the Trinity, then projects can be only means to that end—not ends in themselves. It is the people, and their capacity to maintain healthy relationships with each other, who are the end.

Edward realized that people building is the point of it all. His youth group was somewhat passive, unenthusiastic, and heavily dependent on adult volunteers for their programming. So he did an asset-mapping exercise with the youth. They used their asset cards to generate eight unique ministry ideas. Among them were a car-and-pet wash to raise money for a local animal shelter and a video game-a-thon to raise money for children in Iraq. According to Edward, the effect of the exercise was energizing:

> Youth became excited by the prospect of doing constructive things for the sake of others in their local and global community, provided they were allowed to decide how this would be done. Thus empowered, some of these youth began to ask questions about why they weren't being offered more things to do by church leaders.

Keeping people building as one's focus changes the way leadership is exercised. At times our seminary interns would be tempted to take over a project, circumventing the longer, often frustrating process of teaching people the skills they need in order to get the project done. When they did, the project inevitably had little lasting impact on the congregation.

Of course, it is not easy to "equip the saints for . . . ministry," as Ephesians 4 puts it. If one sees the project as the end, as the real goal, building skills for leadership and communal planning seems inefficient. And it can be very frustrating. A key leader can drop out because of family needs. Conflict between participants on the best way to proceed can paralyze the process. A pastor or parish matriarch may be tempted to swoop in and rescue the project. It puts them in the role of savior and brings satisfaction in seeing plans completed. But the project isn't the point; the people are. Their capacity to invent, cooperate, adapt, and persist must be kept at the forefront. Kristin describes her joy in seeing that happen: "It was thrilling to watch the group as excitement grew and they took ownership of the project. One participant described my role [in the project] as being 'the ghost in the background.'"

Even God doesn't treat community building as the effort of a lone hero. One person of the Trinity doesn't design and build while the others watch or put on finishing touches. All participate equally. "Let *us* make" suggests a cooperative venture. Even God is not in this alone. Creation takes consultation and conversation.

It is not always easy to trust the self-organizing capacity of human beings (and other created things), as I described it in the first chapter. But it is astonishing and faith building to watch people come together in a process like asset mapping, discover that they can create something wonderful, and make it happen.

CHAPTER 5

Beyond Strength

Mobilizing Weakness in the Economy of God

It may seem that "strong" congregations would be less interested in the tools I have been describing. The processes are simple, unassuming, easily mastered. And they may seem unnecessary to the strong. Why bother with an appreciative inquiry to discern God's presence when God's presence is obvious in the large numbers attending one's programs? Who needs to map and mobilize non-financial assets when one's financial coffers are full? These tools could seem to be the last resort of struggling congregations, discouraged leaders, and weak communities. And certainly they can be life transforming in those contexts.

However, the tools are not just a repair kit for damaged or discouraged congregations. Rather, they help all congregations, large and small, reexamine some of their basic assumptions about strength in ministry and community. In fact, the tools rely on the assumption that strength is *not* something to be prized if it is defined simply as self-sufficiency, large size, or financial stability. Such a definition excludes the vast range of ministry potential that comes from partnering with a community, mobilizing all assets, and trusting the power of God.

These tools draw inspiration from the story of Israel and of Jesus and the church. That story describes a people who are anything but big, self-sufficient, and stable. It tells of God's presence revealed *most clearly* in places where structures have cracked or broken, where traditional supports collapse. Unfortunately, this narrative of unexpected strength hidden beneath human weakness, which ought to beat at the heart of our church life, seems underappreciated by church boards and is not often raised at congregational meetings.

A Story of Weakness

The countercultural character of the history Christians cherish was brought home to me when I visited Israel in the spring of 2011. As a Canadian, I experienced it as a miniature country. Israel's entire geography fits between the city in which I live and the next large town north of us in Saskatchewan. The Jordan *River*—deep, wide, and cold, according to the choruses I've sung all my life—turns out to be a *creek* of a size that would not appear on most Canadian maps. It is perhaps five yards wide, a couple deep at most, and as warm as you'd expect in that hot Middle East climate. The *Sea* of Galilee has barely 2 percent of the surface area of the largest lake in our province, which itself is less than 10 percent of Canada's largest lake. Old Jerusalem (especially the first-century section) is no more than a fifteen-minute walk across.

Even today, in spite of modern Israeli roads and buildings, little is glorious about the country when one compares it to the great cities or wonders of the world. Much of the southern half of rural Israel would be little but sand and rock if it weren`t for the occasional olive grove and the square acres of date palms that explode incongruously out of the ground where modern kibbutzim have grown up. Natural resources or tourist attractions, apart from its religious history, are few.

Though I had known these things beforehand intellectually, actually experiencing the country left me with a feeling that I had been duped by the church. Clearly Christianity started as the story of *small* places and small groups of people who for the most part were relatively poor and often refugees from large political conflicts being played out by greater powers surrounding them. Yet we have invested these stories with an artificial—and fraudulent— grandeur that badly distorts the narrative. Jerusalem is peppered with large cathedrals built to commemorate the events of Jesus's life. Yet when one climbs down through the accumulated layers to the ancient setting, one finds little more than a rocky alcove where Jesus's body may have lain or his head rested. Those cathedrals are echoed and exceeded around the world by Willow Creek–type megachurches and the European remnants of the Holy Roman Empire. In my opinion, for too many centuries in too many places, the glorious superstructure of the church that claims the name of Jesus has reflected little of the simple story in which it is supposedly rooted.

Perhaps we have transfigured the story from a sense of shame. After all, as I said in chapter 1, our founder was born out of wedlock. He was homeless, a refugee for several of his early years, and in his latter years he was an itinerant teacher dependent on the welfare of women. Most scandalously, as a prison chaplain reminded me, Jesus and all the apostles except John were convicted of capital crimes, imprisoned, and executed; and John was exiled. In truth, our religion was founded by a band of criminals!

Not surprisingly, the early Christians were not revered; they were mocked. The crucifixion of Jesus was no noble martyr's death. It was shameful, contemptible torture. So when the first Christians told others that their Lord was a crucified man, they were ridiculed. Early Roman graffiti pictured a Christian as a man on his knees praying to a jackass on a cross.[1]

Judeans who believed that God would send a Messiah like King David to renew Israel's worship, to help them throw off the yoke of Rome and bring Israel to its promised greatness, saw this crucified man as a mockery of such hopes. This tortured man a king? This blasphemer would bring renewed worship of God? This helpless victim is supposed to lead Israel to glory? It was ridiculous.

Even those who called themselves Christians had a hard time accepting Jesus's crucifixion. Those who'd caught a tantalizing glimpse of the reign of God in his ministry, who experienced moments when the fundamentals of physics, culture, and faith shifted around him, were deeply disillusioned by Jesus's crucifixion. One who had taken such an active role in challenging the oppressive powers of his world became just another victim of those powers.[2]

And the resurrection only made the problem worse. As Jürgen Moltmann notes in *The Way of Jesus Christ*, Jesus's resurrection forced his followers to face the truth that their first suspicions
were correct—that Jesus is indeed the Messiah. But that simply
heightens the mystery: why, for God's sake, did the Christ have to
suffer and die such a shameful death?[3]

Turned into a Story of the Strong

For almost three hundred years, that sense of shame dogged
Christians as they met in catacombs and homes, endured periods
of persecution, and grew largely by word of mouth. But all that
changed when General Constantine, in the middle of a battle at
Milvian Bridge in 312 CE, looked up to the sun and saw a cross
of light above it, along with the Greek words Εν Τουτω Νικα ("By
this, conquer!"). He commanded his troops to adorn their shields
with the Chi Rho (a symbol for Christ). When he won the battle and claimed for himself the emperor's throne in the West, he
attributed his success to Christ. In keeping with his victory and
grand position, Constantine transmogrified faith in Christ into a
banner for the empire's ambitions to power, size, and public glory.

For the next 1,700-plus years, there was little patience in the
church for weakness, at least among its leaders and in much of
its theology. The church has certainly had an intense aversion to
public shame, especially in modern times. The repression of sexual scandal is a well-known example. The constant fracturing of
church bodies to maintain various kinds of doctrinal, racial, or
ethical purity is another.

But today, despite valiant efforts to maintain its strength, the
Constantinian church in the West is waning. Now that ancient
shame, once masked with gold leaf, shows its troubling face again
as the gilding flakes off. Small or shrinking congregations feel the
shame particularly because they share the pervasive, almost un-
shakeable belief that the presence of God in the church is demonstrated by size and power. They see themselves forgotten by God.

Perhaps one of the most destructive elements of the Constantinian inheritance has been the transformation of the Western

church's core identity. Once composed of the "chosen weak" of 1 Corinthians 1, now it is composed of the "strong" who take care of the poor. The poor who once *constituted* the body of Christ at its center were tossed out to become *objects of its charity* living on its margins.

In my own context this shift is clearly visible in the way in which the aboriginal population has been treated in Canada. From 1600 to almost 1900, European immigrants to Canada depended heavily upon the hospitality, transportation network, economic structures, justice processes, agricultural, and survival wisdom of the First Nations living in the land. Still today, many things Canadians most prize about their culture were gifts from the First Nations, not from Britain or France.[4]

But once Europeans established themselves, the immigrants' attitude changed. Native economic and political competition was restricted by confining First Nations people to reserves; they could not leave without a pass and could not sell produce without a permit, both given at the discretion of Indian agents. The bison, millions strong and the primary source of food and clothing on the prairies, were virtually wiped out by European hide hunters, leaving Native bands starving.

And the churches in Canada joined in the power grab. Though their pews had once been populated primarily by full-blood Natives and Métis, they decided that their First Nations members were not really ministers but objects of ministry. They needed to be "civilized," cared for, reeducated, put on welfare—essentially infantilized. Residential schools were established by the government and run mostly (though not exclusively) by churches, forcing Native children away from their families. The schools stripped them of their language, their own spiritual traditions (often a mixture of traditional and Christian), their clothing, their familial relations.

The result has been chaos. A once proud and capable people have been dealt a severe blow. In Canadian prairie cities like Winnipeg, Saskatoon, and Regina, the faces of the poor, imprisoned, homeless, and addicted are disproportionately those of First Nations people.

Ironically, however, in the process of ejecting its "weak" aboriginal people, the Canadian church among those of European descent has dwindled in energy and outreach. And, as happened in many places in the United States in African American communities, the gospel of God's presence among the disregarded has been appropriated by many Native churches that, under their own leadership, are comparatively flourishing.

The Weakness of Strength

A serious flaw in the "bigger, stronger, faster" philosophy that has afflicted the church is that it fosters a survival-of-the-fittest climate in which fitness is understood to increase with size and income. So members of small churches live in fear of being closed ("murdered," "given the axe," I've heard it called). They are afraid they will lose the worship fellowship they have come to depend on. They won't have any place to be married or buried. And they face the shame of no longer being able to bear the flag of their denomination and the iconic presence of God in their community. The fear can turn them inward, away from the communities and the mission God has given them.

Oddly, the question about their future is not whether small churches *can* survive. Thousands of rural churches in North America have lived a century or two or three through a host of community changes. In all that time, most have never been large. Rather, survival-of-the-fittest thinking assumes that weak (generally defined as small and financially poor) churches don't *deserve* to live.

This moral judgment rests on two assumptions. The first is that money is the lifeblood of the church—its one true foundation. In spite of the fact that churches all over the world, in Asia, Africa, Latin America, flourish with little or no cash, North Americans have bought capitalism's assurance that nothing good happens without money. Income gives life; nothing holds out hope for the future like a flush bank account. Of course, membership numbers matter, too, because unless a church has a wealthy benefactor, more folks in the pews normally means more income.

The second assumption is that church income is a limited, even scarce, resource, because it depends on the generosity of congregants. Therefore only new missions, or those congregations that most clearly demonstrate (by their size and budget) that they are accomplishing the church's mission, ought to be supported by regional church structures.

If scarcity is the mindset, it follows that competition for resources will be inevitable. So churches in the same neighborhood may see themselves as competitors for the limited number of people likely to consider church membership. They may be reluctant to partner with each other. Regional church budgets can become battlegrounds where the largest churches have the loudest voices and greatest influence because they contribute the most.

There are a multitude of problems with this Nietzschean thinking. First of all, by weakening the web of cooperation between churches, it increases a community's suspicion of church-initiated programs. The community may ask, "Are these folks really out to do something for the well-being of everyone, or are they just trying to fill their pews and coffers?" When churches cooperate, the community more easily trusts them.

Second, the philosophy suffers from a means-end inversion. It assumes that churches have *only* instrumental value—that they are tools in the mission of God but are not, in themselves, essential objects of God's love. There is no question that the church has a calling. But the church is called *because it is God's beloved*; it is not loved because it is so effective in its mission. Paul Minear, in his classic work, analyzes ninety-six images of the church in the New Testament.[5] He points out that these images ring not only with affirmations of the church's call and purpose but also with the value of its essential being. "You are a chosen race, a royal priesthood, a holy nation, God's own people," the writer of 1 Peter insists (2:9). "I am the vine, you are the branches," Jesus says of his followers in John 15:5. The church's relationship with God is an intimate one, and the value given it in the New Testament appears to be intrinsic.

Even when Christ scolds the church, as in John's vision in Revelation 2 and 3, there is still a deep underlying tone of love, a yearning to reconnect with these congregations, that implies they cannot simply be discarded. And his critique tends to be not of their weakness but of their arrogance and wealth (see his words to Laodicea in 3:15–22, for example)—those things that would lead the church into independent self-reliance. In fact, his greatest *commendation* is to the *weakest* church, the one in Philadelphia: "I know that you have but little power . . . [but] they will learn that I have loved you" (vv. 8–9).

To marginalize or close churches because they have small numbers and little income would be like a father kicking out his young children because they were too expensive to care for and weren't earning enough money. The children are the point of it all; money is just one means of supporting them. You don't get rid of the children to ease pressure on family resources. You look for other resources, or a different kind of resources, to support the ones you love. And as we have seen in the chapter on asset mapping, an enormous range of resources beyond the monetary is available to churches, most of which are generally unmapped and untapped.

Third, there is a fragility in the concentration of power that a survival-of-the-fittest approach to ministry seeks. When all the church's eggs are held in just a few megachurch baskets, a single devastating event—sexual misconduct by a key leader, for example—can topple a congregation, resulting in the disenfranchisement of thousands. Large entities require an enormous and consistent food supply. A megachurch pastor told me that if they take in less than half a million dollars in offering each week for more than a month, they have to lay off half a dozen staff members.

A fourth problem is the danger of self-delusion. Christ says to the church in Laodicea, "You say, 'I am rich, I have prospered, and I need nothing.' You do not realize that you are wretched, pitiable, poor, blind, and naked" (Rev. 3:17). When a congregation is large and wealthy, members can be lured into believing they have all the resources they need to carry out the mission of God. Instead of acting as catalysts to mobilize the vast array of resources in the community around them, they tend to mount their own programs, depending on the resources they have accumulated and can easily control.

The danger for large congregations (and I have served a couple) is that they may not recognize the difference between power concentrated and power *channeled*. It's like the difference between a battery and a lightning rod. The most impressive collection of industrial batteries can never begin to match the enormous output of electricity drawn up from the earth's vast reservoir and down from massive cloudbanks through a simple lightning rod in a thunderstorm. The weakest church knows it can't supply energy for all the social programs a community needs. But it can be a lightning rod, attracting leadership and energy to coalesce around a core need or interest. Having little power itself at least creates the possibility that a congregation may seek to be a channel or catalyst for the power of the whole community, even the power of God.

Finally, valorizing the "strong" makes it difficult to build a cohesive community. If God's mission is to build communities that reflect something of the life of the Trinity, then failing to build such communities shows that this philosophy is fundamentally opposed to the divine presence in creation—that it is something we might even label *evil*. For in fact, we *have* named as evil those many horrors in the past century perpetrated when the "strong" set out to remove the "weak" entirely through physical or economic genocide.

Strangely, the weak turn out to be an essential binding agent in communities. Strength can breed independence. A group of humans composed entirely of the strong might resemble a box of Lego blocks in which each piece had only bumps—no indentations, and therefore no way to connect to another. They could be called a *collection* but not a *community*. But when one person's gifts and another's needs are connected, community begins to form.

Of course, most times the strong do *not* remove the weak entirely because they depend on them economically. The 2011 Occupy movement insisted that the wealthy 1 percent can only exist because they feed off the excess value of the labor provided by the 99 percent. Certainly our world's capital resources (though certainly not *social* capacities and other key assets) are distributed with astonishing inequity. The Helsinki-based World Institute for Development Economics Research of the United Nations University

(UNU-WIDER) reports that globally 1 percent of adults owned 40 percent of global assets in the year 2000. To belong to this 1 percent required that one control about $500,000 in capital assets.[6] Canada and the United States alone control 34 percent of the world's wealth, though having only 6 percent of its population.

These same inequities exist within North America. Typically they are marked at the community level by geographic boundaries. So we speak of those who live "on the wrong side of the tracks" or those who enjoy the status of life "uptown" among the moneyed. That division gives the impression, to return to our Lego metaphor, that some people have only "bumps" and others have only "indents." While these two groups may interconnect at the level of owner-worker industry or tax-based welfare, it is nothing like the deep integration we have seen in the life of Father, Son, and Spirit.

Within the Trinity the giving is not one way; it's fully reciprocal. The Bible tells of a Father who chooses to be weak, releasing power and control to the Son and Spirit so that they can carry out the divine mission among humans. In his ascension, the Son does the same, leaving an incomplete mission and a frightened band of followers to the care of the Spirit. At the last day, Paul says, the Son and the Spirit will impoverish themselves, offering the creation they have redeemed and sanctified back to the care of the Father.

This sort of reciprocity can form powerful bonds when its possibility is acknowledged. For example, in our context, First Nations and adjacent rural communities have a great deal to offer one another if they could cross the barriers of stereotype and habit that separate them. Those First Nations who have worked hard to heal and rebuild their people are a wonderful repository of wisdom and experience for their non-Native neighbors. They have dealt straight up with problems that tend to be kept under the surface in white or wealthier communities. Among rural youth, for example, drug addiction, alcoholism, and driving underage and under the influence of alcohol or other drugs are widespread, according to research.[7] As I write this, nine teens have been involved in deadly drinking and driving accidents in different locations on the prairies in the past two weeks. One clergyperson told me recently that his small community has come to accept one young person's death on their rural roads almost every year—most involving alcohol. Yet little is being done to address the issues. It brings shame to communities even to publicly admit the problem—of course, thereby preventing the problems from being tackled in an effective way.

But "weaker" communities that have found the courage to face and deal with such issues can, in fact, be saving grace for their "stronger" neighbors. Real honesty is possible in conversation with them. Maintaining "face" isn't necessary, because whatever one might admit, those whose struggles have already been made public aren't likely to judge. And since they've begun to address their own issues, they can suggest where the potholes—and the well-paved sections—in the road might lie.

Best of all, they can model how to do both law and gospel well. One Pentecostal pastor on a First Nations reserve told me of his congregation's work with their young people. Every one of them is repeatedly told in words and actions that they are cared for and valued, regardless of their behavior or addictions. But *because* they are valued, they are also given some strict codes of life to help them stay well. As their church has provided structured support and fulfilling jobs and ministry, as it has challenged destructive behavior but affirmed personal value, they have done some wonderful work in building healthy teens that any church should be proud to emulate.

A final caution about the way in which we understand strength and identify the strong. It is instructive to remember that Jesus wasn't knifed by thugs in a dark alley. He wasn't mugged by a junkie looking for cash. It was the brightest and best of that time who crucified him. He was condemned by the Jewish Sanhedrin— the most respected judges of morality in Judea. He was executed by the best international legal system of his day—the Roman courts. And the laws under which he was condemned were good laws, laws that we still support. There was a religious law prohibiting people from claiming to be God, from blasphemy. It helped to keep cults under control. A good law, surely; but Jesus broke it. There was a law against betraying your country—against treason.

That's a good law, isn't it? But in response to the question about paying taxes, Jesus made it clear that he had loyalties much higher than Caesar, and he threatened Roman rule when he drowned the Romans' food supply (the two thousand pigs). There was a law banning terrorist threats, but Jesus overthrew the tables of the moneychangers in the temple and said that if the temple was torn down, he would rebuild it in three days. Blasphemy, treason, and terrorist threats. Jesus was judged guilty of these crimes by some of the best institutions, the greatest human wisdom and learning of his day. But that judgment turned out to be so wrong. In God's economy, our strength can be our greatest weakness.

The Strength of Weakness

Conversely, there can be a profound strength in those we assume are weak. Paul talks about the dynamics of weakness in his own life. His autobiography in 2 Corinthians 11:24–30 is anything but a trophy case of victories:

> Five times I have received from the Jews the forty lashes minus one. Three times I was beaten with rods. Once I received a stoning. Three times I was shipwrecked; for a night and a day I was adrift at sea; on frequent journeys, in danger from rivers, danger from bandits, danger from my own people, danger from Gentiles, danger in the city, danger in the wilderness, danger at sea, danger from false brothers and sisters; in toil and hardship, through many a sleepless night, hungry and thirsty, often without food, cold and naked. And, besides other things, I am under daily pressure because of my anxiety for all the churches. Who is weak, and I am not weak? Who is made to stumble, and I am not indignant?

Yet, at the end of this litany of woes, Paul concludes, "If I must boast, I will boast of the things that show my weakness." How strange.

Paul doesn't come to this bizarre form of boasting easily. He refers to a physical disability (sight-related perhaps) that particularly haunted him: "Three times I appealed to the Lord about this, that it would leave me." God's response however was clear: "But he said to me, 'My grace is sufficient for you, for power is made perfect in weakness.'" Out of that assurance Paul is then able to say, "I will boast all the more gladly of my weaknesses, so that the power of Christ may dwell in me. Therefore I am content with weaknesses, insults, hardships, persecutions, and calamities for the sake of Christ; for whenever I am weak, then I am strong" (2 Cor. 12:8–10).

There is a story whose origins I have forgotten about a man who asks his rabbi, "Why does God write the law *on* our hearts? Why not *in* our hearts? It's the inside of my heart that needs God." The rabbi answered, "God never forces anything into a human heart. He writes the word on our hearts so that when our hearts break, God falls in." That was certainly Paul's experience during his blindness on the Damascus road and throughout his difficult ministry. His unguarded broken heart became a sponge to absorb the presence of God.

I believe that the same can be said for congregations and communities. When the structures that we rely upon for ministry crumble, it's then that God may "fall in" to do something new and potentially transformative.

HOW THE POWER OF GOD
OPERATES IN HUMAN WEAKNESS

How does this divine power really work? What is the evidence that God's "power is made perfect in weakness"? Is this just Paul's consolation prize, or is it a paradigm for life? And how would it work in a community setting? Let's look at several possibilities.

Holey Ministry Can Reveal the Holy

Paul says "We have this treasure [the knowledge of God] in *clay jars* [weak vessels], so that it may be made clear that this extraordinary power belongs to God and does not come from us" (2 Cor. 4:7, italics mine). I noted in chapter 3 that the New Testament speaks about *charisms*—gifts of the Spirit—in a way that implies that the Holy Spirit fills us or "puts us on," almost like a glove. Filled by the Spirit, the church accomplishes more than one might expect. When the church is visibly strong or wealthy, those accomplishments may simply be attributed to the church itself. But when the glove clearly has holes in it, when the church helps something to happen that it clearly could not have accomplished in its own power, then the community is more likely to say, "We did it together" or even "God was at work here."

A community that can see God at work in its midst has a true hope, an unassailable hope. Its hopes aren't pinned on charismatic leaders, highly skilled organizers, or exceptional institutions—all of which can leave, be dismantled, or be overwhelmed by stronger powers from outside. But when a community's members discover that God is at work among them, there is never reason to give up. They can say with Paul, "We are afflicted in every way, but not crushed; perplexed, but not driven to despair" (2 Cor. 4:8). Knowing that God is there, they know that the door to their future is open. And so it is worth working for change, trying new things, or just trying again.

Our Weakness Can Foster Strength in Others

"Nature abhors a vacuum" is a principle that sometimes (not always) applies in community development when leaders leave space for the strengths of others to step in. That's what happened in the Hindu village that I spoke about in chapter 1. Wealthy NGOs came into the village to fix their problems. The villagers admired them and came to depend on the wealth they brought. But when the NGOs left and the last check ran out, all the benefits they had brought were lost. It wasn't until a church agency came that had little or no money to give, just a knack for stimulating conversation and helping people discover their own resources, that the village was able to build a permanent, sustainable recovery. They said, "Others had always done it for us—but now we've discovered we can do it ourselves!" The agency engaged the villagers from a position of apparent weakness (financially at least), working behind the scenes to foster interdependence among the villagers, rather than dependence on the agency.

The Weak Can Stir Up a Community's Passions

While it is not inevitable—for the weak can be agents of chaos and invite scorn—a community in which the church is doing its part to welcome and honor the weak can become a passionate place. Several examples might help to illustrate.

CHILDREN
Until my wife and I had our first child, I had little sense of what it meant to *serve*. As a bachelor, even as a newly married man, I was mostly concerned about my own needs and agenda. But our first baby was helpless. My wife and I had to do everything for him, around the clock. We fed and clothed him, amused him, hauled him around, wiped his tears, and cleaned off the vile stuff he kept spitting out of other cavities in his body. But it has been good for me. In the process of caring for children, I have learned to share, to be patient, to be a servant, to be hospitable.

Children do the same for a community. By their very helplessness they draw people out of their insulated lives to build schools, coach baseball, cook meals, and give piano lessons. Children stir up in us a nurturing compassion that leads us into Christ's servant life. In the process, they also connect us to one another. All that caretaking requires conversation and organization. Adult friendships form in school PTA meetings. Economic partnerships develop at the hockey rink. The community knits together around children's needs.

Children also teach us how to do sabbath. Sabbath is about play and rest and delight in things. These, someone has said, are the serious work of eternity; we keep a sabbath time here as a way of practicing for the new creation. That's where children shine. You don't meet many workaholic kids. When they were young, mine had a strong interest in play and a fair resistance to work. And though they generated work for us, they also drew us into their play and for a while helped us lose our adult worries in the simple joy of children's games. Our children also knew how to rest—anywhere, anytime, though not necessarily when we wanted them to. I recall our eldest eating breakfast, forging his way through a huge bowl of oatmeal, and then, as he slowed down, his head would start to nod, and next thing you know, he would be fast asleep with his face in the bowl—"feeling his oats," I suppose.

And there is so much that delights children. They squeal with laughter because the world is new to them and full of surprises. They run to us and invite us to see it through their eyes. We learn how to delight in the world again, to see God in it again. With children, we learn to play, and we learn to rest with them, because we know that when they wake, we will have a lot of caring and playing to do.

Jesus said, "It is to such as these [little children] that the kingdom of heaven belongs. Truly I tell you, whoever does not receive the kingdom of God as a little child will never enter it" (Mark 10:15). Babies show us *how to receive God*—by simply trusting, unresistant. Their helplessness reveals the essence of our relationship to God: God is the potter, we are the clay; God is the source, we are the expression. Babies trust God, they allow God to care for them, they don't even try to manage on their own. They let God be God, as Luther says.

The prophet Isaiah foretold, "A little child shall lead them" (11:6). In a survival-of-the-fittest paradigm, these weakest ones could be seen as little more than parasites. But in practice, and in many more ways than I have described, the Spirit works through them to make our communities strong. They don't simply ensure the continuance of the community (its future); they hold it together *now*.

SUFFERERS
Paul says in Galatians, "You know that it was because of [or "through"] a physical infirmity that I first announced the gospel to you; though my condition put you to the test, you did not scorn or despise me, but welcomed me as an angel of God, as Christ Jesus" (4:13–14). Love often expresses itself best through

sufferers. In fact, love and suffering are linked in English by the term *passion*. Passion can refer to the desire one has for another: a man is passionate about his lover. It can refer to the anger that is aroused when love perceives an injustice: "the heat of passion." And we speak of the "passion of Christ" in our liturgies to refer to the pains Jesus suffered in his last days. Desire, anger, and pain—all these expressions of passion are aroused when a congregation gives sufferers visibility.

I had an experience of passion aroused in a congregation by sufferers during my doctoral research. Interviewing people about the social and spiritual dynamics of farm bankruptcy, I became accustomed to hearing expressions of shame from those who were struggling financially. But one town expressed very little of that. When I asked why, I was told that the change in social climate had grown out of an incident at a congregational meeting. The pastor, a former banker, had been secretly accompanying farmers to their debt review meetings to ensure that they were treated fairly. But at his church's annual meeting, some criticized the pastor for spending so much time with these "poor managers" and not enough time looking after the congregation. They assumed that "good Lutherans" wouldn't get into that sort of trouble. During a break in the meeting the pastor took some of the young adults aside for a talk. When the meeting resumed, some of them got up and said, "Those 'bad managers' that the pastor has been working with—that's us." Suddenly the frame flipped. These were beloved children of the congregation; they couldn't just be dismissed as inept, and their suffering couldn't be scorned from a distance. The congregation was plunged into their young adults' financial struggles. Over a few months, it became a more passionate place in several ways. They felt a more poignant love for these members in need, a wound in their own hearts as the other members shared their pain, and a growing anger at economic conditions and government policies that made it so difficult for young people to take up farming. That passion expressed itself in "farmgate" defense actions, in signs posted down the highways and at the provincial legislature, and in community forums where those having various roles in farm bankruptcy were able to share their perspectives. They mobilized other congregations in the area to create conversations between farmers and town businesses, whose economic well-being was linked. While no farmers were outed in this process, the mantle of secrecy was removed and the suffering was borne together. That region became a more passionate place as they repented, lamented, and protested together.

Love and suffering cannot be separated. We not only suffer *with* those we love, we also suffer *them*. I told my wife before we got married, "If you love me, honey, you're going to suffer." She married me anyway, but with eyes open, knowing she was getting a man who was absentminded, a bit cerebral, and sometimes insensitive. She knew that if she opened her heart to me, she was going to get hurt. I would forget some anniversary, forget to turn off the stove, belittle her feelings, or worse. And I have. But she is a passionate woman. For forty years she has loved me enough to bear the suffering I've caused her. Such passionate love makes tolerance and reconciliation possible in our homes and communities.

And sufferers can lead us to Christ. In the parable in Matthew 25:34–40, the king says, "I was hungry . . . thirsty . . . a stranger . . . naked . . . sick . . . in prison," and "You gave me food . . . drink . . . clothing . . . , you took care of me . . . , you visited me." When the listeners are baffled, certain they had never done such things for the king, he says, "Truly I tell you, as you did it to one of the least of these who are members of my family, you did it to me." Moltmann says that sufferers introduce us to the double "brotherhood" or double "apostolate" of Christ.[8] When we engage someone who is suffering, we may imagine that we are bringing them Jesus, even *being* Christ for them. And so we are. The surprise is that in them we also meet our suffering Lord. They are Christ for us.

I remember being called to Amy's bedside in the middle of the night. She was close to death, and her children wanted a pastor. When I got there, Amy was in some pain, clearly uncomfortable. But she smiled when she saw me. I asked her how she was coping. She said, "It hurts." I asked her if death frightened her. She said, "Sure. . . . I've no idea what death will be like. But Jesus has been through it. He knows. He's been there for me my whole life. I guess he'll see me through death, too." I shared Jesus with Amy and her family but nothing like the way she shared Jesus with me. In her pain and fear, she introduced me to the Jesus of Gethsemane and the cross. And in her trust, she led me to the Christ who conquered death. I discovered that the fellowship of the healthy and the hurting is one fellowship—embraced by our crucified and risen Savior.

OFFENDERS

After one of my children was assaulted randomly several times in a three-month period, I realized that police cannot keep us safe. It takes the whole community to hold its people accountable and keep them within the bounds of love and law. So I became a volunteer chaplain at our two local prisons. It has been an eye-opening experience. Before I had any direct contact with prisoners, I had many noble ideas about the justice system, its fairness and effectiveness. But those have been largely dashed in conversation with prisoners. For example, I always assumed that prison sentences had some effect on deterring crime. But one day I was visiting a young man accused of murder. He said to me, "I voted for the first time today." "Who did you vote for?" I asked. "Well, not that guy who says he's tough on crime!" I smiled, thinking I knew his reasons. But he went on, "You know why? Because he thinks that longer sentences will keep people like us from offending. But most of the crimes in my family were committed when we were drunk or high. None of us was thinking, 'I wonder if I should steal that car, considering the fact that the sentence for theft has gone up by six months.' We don't even know what the sentences are. This guy has no idea what our lives are like. Fighting, getting drunk, no place to stay. If those politicians were really tough on crime, they'd do more about the tough problems that land us in here. They're not tough on crime; they're lazy. Lock 'em up! That's their only solution."

When offenders are sealed off from our society so we have little or no interaction with them, then the real dynamics of community safety, and the real causes of violence, are hidden. Whether we like it or not, the only ones who can truly educate us about what works and doesn't work in community safety are offenders themselves and the people who know them well.

In chaplaincy work, I also discovered that our system of "objective" justice can be experienced as *immoral* by offenders. This is how it sometimes looks to those charged with a first offense. Let's say that Bob has assaulted Mark and badly injured him. Most likely Bob has known Mark for some time. They may even be friends or relatives. After the assault, Bob may be feeling bad about what he has done to Mark and want to patch things up. But he has no chance. Strong folks with guns (police)—whom Bob has never injured in any way—come and do bad things to Bob. They kidnap him, lock him up, threaten him, put him in a concrete box with violent people, and give him little access to family and friends. They feed him lousy food and bring him in front of a bunch of rich, educated people who talk quietly about him in language he can't really understand and then send him back to the box for a long time. Meanwhile, Bob is completely cut off from Mark and Mark's family, with no possibility of repairing the relationship that he damaged. Bob feels as though he is prevented from fixing the problem he caused and is simultaneously being mistreated by strangers whom he has never hurt.

That perspective was new to me. Hearing it from prisoners has led churches to support *restorative justice* movements aimed first at healing relationships and not simply punishing (taking state revenge on) prisoners. It has also challenged me and many others to take our own relationships more seriously. We learn moral discernment and courage when these weak ones are not simply locked up (though, clearly, some need that restraint) but are allowed to have some proper voice in our communities. And I say this as a father whose children have been innocent victims of violent crimes.

In Gideon's Life

Judges 7 recounts how Gideon encountered God's unconventional way of working through the weak to strengthen his people. The Midianite army was camped on Israel's doorstep. As Israel's warrior-leader, Gideon figured the only way to fend off their enemies was to raise a huge army, so he recruited thirty-two thousand men. But listen to what God tells Gideon in Judges 7:2:

> The LORD said to Gideon, "The troops with you are *too many* for me to give the Midianites into their hand. [How often do you hear "too many" from the Pentagon, or our pastors?] *Israel would only take the credit away from me, saying, 'My own hand has delivered me.'* Now therefore proclaim this in the hearing of the troops, 'Whoever is fearful and trembling, let him return home.'" Thus Gideon sifted them out; twenty-two thousand returned, and ten thousand remained. Then the LORD said to Gideon, "The troops are *still too many*; take them down to the water and I will sift them out for you there. When I say, 'This one shall go with you,' he shall go with you; and when I say, 'This one shall not go with you,' he shall not go." So he brought the troops down to the water; and the LORD said to Gideon, "All those who lap the water with their tongues, as a dog laps, you shall put to one side; all those who kneel down to drink, putting their hands to their mouths, you shall put to the other side." The number of those that lapped was three hundred; but all the rest of the troops knelt down to drink water. Then the LORD said to Gideon, "With the three hundred that lapped I will deliver you, and give the Midianites into your hand. Let all the others go to their homes" (italics mine).

You may know the rest of the story: those three hundred musicians walked into the Midianite camp at night with nothing in their hands but a trumpet, a torch, and a clay jar covering the light. They spread out through the camp, then pulled the jars off the torches and blew the trumpets. The Midianites, thinking the Israelites were attacking at night, jumped up, and not being able to see in the dark, fought each other. Then the Lord put fear in their hearts and they ran.

The approach that Gideon and the three hundred took was unorthodox, of course. It had to be; they couldn't use a large army's methods and resources. Gideon's guerrilla "band" had to give up on swords and shields and look for other weapons. It took

imaginative asset mapping and a lot of guts, but they saved Israel
with lamps, clay pots, and musical instruments. A most unexpected victory.

Why did God prefer that commando unit to a big army? Because Israel's only hope in that hostile world was to depend on
God. If they started to believe that their hope was in the number
of their soldiers or the sophistication of their armory, they were
doomed. They would be cut to pieces by Babylon or Assyria or
Egypt. And they would cut themselves off from God. God *insisted
on smallness* so that their *only hope* would be in God and so they
would understand that *all* life, every aspect and artifact, has potential for mission in the hands of God.

North Americans need to hear that. There is an independent
streak that runs through our societies. Perhaps left over from pio-
neer settlement myths,[9] many of us like to believe that we are self-
reliant people, capable of managing our own lives, *in control.* We
can forget that God is the source of our life and that we need each
other. It is easier to remember those things when we are small or
weak.

It's not just that smallness creates conditions in which we may
be open to divine assistance. The biblical stories hide a secret not
well recognized even by those who claim it as their sacred history:
most significant change begins small. Jesus tells it in parable form
in Matthew 13:31–33:

> The kingdom of heaven is like a mustard seed that someone took
> and sowed in his field; it is the smallest of all the seeds, but when
> it has grown it is the greatest of shrubs and becomes a tree, so that
> the birds of the air come and make nests in its branches. He told
> them another parable: The kingdom of heaven is like yeast that a
> woman took and mixed in with three measures of flour until all
> of it was leavened.

Yeast and seeds. That's what our small congregations are. Not
dying patients in a palliative care ward. Not the fossilized bones
of once-mammoth congregations. They are God's yeast growing
new life in their communities. They are God's seed saved from

an old harvest, offered to their community as the start of a new crop.

The Gifts of Small Congregations

In the concluding section I will share a few of the gifts I have found that weak congregations—particularly those small in size—can offer to the mission of God. I have to say first, however, that these gifts are not well acknowledged by small congregations themselves, let alone their communities and denominational structures.

As part of my work in community development, I have visited many small congregations over the last ten years. A lot of them reside in rural communities that are themselves struggling (though it is also true of many inner city settings). Some towns close to large cities are being amalgamated. Their voices are lost in the noise of urban concerns, their identity and services leached away by the city's magnetic influence. Mining, lumber, fishing, cattle, and crop communities are distressed by boom and bust cycles—mostly the latter right now. They are losing their livelihood to mountain pine beetles, cod-stock overfishing, BSE (bovine spongiform encephalopathy, or "mad-cow disease"), drought, and trade disputes. Tourist towns struggle with seasonal income. Nonresidents buy up homes as summer cottages, pushing property taxes and house prices higher than young families can afford. And most rural communities lament the loss of their youth in general. Rural kids have always left to go to school or to see the world for a while, but now they are not coming back.

The congregations in these town and country settings are often equally stressed: their church membership is dwindling; the long-time organist left, and they can't get a new one; there are lots of empty pews; the Sunday school has folded; money is tight; and a full-time pastor is a distant memory. A pall of depression settles over these communities and congregations. The glass they hold up is, in their minds, almost empty. What they often don't see is that in their shrinking size, they are being prepared for a new way of doing ministry.

Small Places *May* Do Well At . . .

Below are some of the things smallness may allow congregations to do well. Note, however, that smallness does not *in itself* ensure these effects. The mustard seed in Jesus's parable could not of itself grow into "the *greatest* of shrubs." It takes a power (God's) not contained in the seed. Similarly, the *power of God* at work in open hearts is what gives the small and weak an impact disproportionate to their size.

ALLOWING EVERYONE'S GIFTS TO BE OPENED

I've sat in many small congregations and listened to a young flute player or vocalist share their musical talents in worship. It's easier because the atmosphere is less formal. In larger places people assume that only the most skilled performers should be up front, and there are lots of those, so the young and novice get little opportunity to share their gifts. In a large congregation, people may not even offer. They think, "Well there's someone else who can do this better." In a small church, you know there may not be anyone else who can do it at all—so you've got to step up to the plate. So smallness helps bring out hidden gifts.

ENSURING PEOPLE FEEL THAT THEY,
AND THEIR PARTICIPATION, MATTER

A higher percentage of small church members tend to be in worship each Sunday than in larger churches; they know they will be missed. They tend to be more generous, per person, in their giving, because they know their contribution will be noted and it will have a greater impact on the overall budget of the congregation. When I did a survey in urban churches in Toronto, I discovered that the leadership of these larger congregations had come, disproportionately, from small rural churches. These folks had moved into the city, joined a church, and heard the announcement, "We need Sunday school teachers and council members." Having been formed in a congregation where everyone was expected to do their part, they stepped up to the plate and volunteered. So our big urban churches depended on leadership formed in small, often rural, congregations!

CONNECTING ON A PERSONAL LEVEL

This is possible in several arenas of church ministry, particularly worship and caregiving. In worship, if the congregation numbers in the hundreds, people are relatively faceless. The minister can really only preach *at* them. Among a hundred or so, she might know enough individuals to begin to preach *to* the people. At fifty or fewer, the preacher can begin to *talk with* her people, getting them some space to talk back. But with a dozen or so, it is possible to have a genuine heart-to-heart conversation. There is room for the sharing of individual faith stories and experiences—what we used to call testimonies.

Regarding caregiving, it is much easier to find out each other's business in small churches. The gossip travels quickly. That can lead to shame and misery if people are judgmental. But it can lead to wonderful caring if they are hospitable and compassionate. The terms *hospital* and *hospitality* come from the Latin word *hospes,* meaning "host." When we host others, we open our hearts to them, we open our time to them, we open our wallets to them. We become willing to give and to receive from them. In a large church there are so many people that one may hesitate to open one's heart in a public setting for fear of being overwhelmed. But in a small place, there aren't so many. It is possible to keep track of who is sick, who has time to visit, who needs encouragement, guidance, or intervention. So small places can be better at lending a hand directly to someone who needs it; they are right-sized to be up-close and personal.

As we saw in chapter 1, this sort of vulnerable hospitality characterizes the life that Father, Son, and Spirit share with each other. The technical theological jargon for it is *perichoresis* or *circumincessio.* It means living within each other, or interweaving one's lives like macramé, like an intricate dance. However, it does take courage. Small churches are not good places for those who want to be anonymous. People in small churches may put up firm walls to protect their privacy. They know that being vulnerable *will* mean getting hurt; there's no question about that. Jesus's openness to the Father resulted in great pain when he couldn't sense the Father's presence on the cross. "My God, why have you forsaken me?" If such pain can happen inside the Trinity, who love each other so dearly, it will surely happen in small groups when people open up to each other. When we share our needs, some people will respond in ways that aren't helpful even if they intend to be. Others, when they are hurt or angry, will use our vulnerabilities against us—attacking our soft spots. So to be a hospital, a place of hospitality, a small congregation has to have courage, a commitment to loving even through hurts, and a regular practice of confession, absolution, and reconciliation.

This is true in the relationship with their pastors too. Small churches can have very close relationships with their clergy. Pastors who love their people in small congregations usually get a lot of love in return. But if they hurt their people, or are hurt by them, there can be a lot more pain.

GETTING THINGS DONE

When the Spirit moves someone in a small church to start something, that person has far fewer barriers to overcome. There is less red tape, fewer people who need to be convinced. Individuals generally have more influence. Bigger churches have a lot of inertia. It takes time and push to get them going. Of course, small churches can bog down because one or two people are strongly opposed to something; there is more of a concern for consensus. But they can also make quick decisions. I was present at a worship service when a congregation member said, during the announcements, "That outside west wall is starting to look kind of shabby. Who will join me next Saturday to give it a coat of paint?" Several hands went up, and by the following Sunday it was done. In a bigger place, that process could have taken weeks or months of consultations and contractor bids. Similarly, I have seen small churches mobilize rapidly to deal with floods, sickness and death, and a variety of other community crises. Smaller groups can be flexible and responsive. They tend to respond to the concrete, which means that giving to general expenses may not always be high. But in a crunch, the practical need to put on a new roof or to build a long-term care facility or to help a family whose house burned down can allow money and labor to come in quickly and generously.

CONNECTING THE GENERATIONS

This can happen in a couple of ways. First, smaller churches may find it easier to remember their history. There are simply fewer events and people to remember, so the history is easier to pass on. The exploits of a fabled matriarch, the lightning strike that hit the church, the favorite hymns of Mrs. Jones who had sole custody of the organ for twenty-five years are all remembered, retold, re-sung. Churches in town-and-country settings may have the additional advantage of a cemetery outside the sanctuary where the ancestors' names and dates are constantly on display. It's easier in such places to talk about the "God of Abraham, Isaac, and Jacob"—or "the God of Ole, Morgan, and Lois."

Second, in large churches, like one I served, each age group had its own organizations, and they didn't mix much. Smaller churches don't face that temptation. Christian education, for example, tends to happen in multigraded classes. Evidence from secular education studies indicates that the learning in such classes can be better.[10] Students are less likely to be passive absorbers of information. They have to actively integrate it so they can help younger students, and in the process they learn by teaching. Apart from education, almost any activity that requires a significant number of people will draw on more than one age group in small churches. It makes adult-child relationships and responsibilities more comfortable. It fosters understanding of other generations. And in the adolescent years, when peer competition is high, it can be a saving grace for students to have strong connections to people younger and older than themselves.

RETAINING MEMBERS

In small groups, people notice when members are absent. In a large church I served, people sometimes said, "I suppose you're wondering why I wasn't here last Sunday." I never had the heart to tell them that, out of one-thousand-plus members, there was no way for me to tell that they hadn't been present. Small churches, on the other hand, may be difficult to get into and feel accepted. But if they genuinely welcome new folks and adopt them into their family, it is not easy for those folks to leave. They know they'll be missed. People ask how they're doing. Ties and friendships develop that hold them close. I remember talking to a man in a small suburban church who was very unhappy with the pastor's theology. I asked him why he stayed. He looked at me for a moment, then reached over and grasped the hand of a frail woman nearby. "Mary would miss me," he said. "I pick her up for worship each Sunday. And my daughter teaches Sunday school." Like a net, friendship and mutual responsibility kept him there.

CELEBRATING THE RHYTHMS OF LIFE
IN CHURCH AND COMMUNITY

Birthdays, graduations, special honors, and anniversaries can be publicly celebrated in smaller churches. In smaller communities or inner city neighborhoods, it is common for churches to be actively involved in local festivals, work bees, community fund-raising, and other events. Because the life passages of church and community members are better known, it is easier for small congregations to help folks navigate the joys and sorrows of those changes.

FORGING COMMUNITY AND
ECUMENICAL PARTNERSHIPS

Large churches with many internal resources can often function quite independently in a community. But a small church knows that if they are to get anything done, they will have to work with the Baptists, Lutherans, or Catholics down the street or the staff at the long-term care facility or the town council. They know that they need others, and so they may help to form the interdependent community that reflects God's own communal life. In the process, they also develop community credibility, because their willingness to partner suggests that they care about the community's well-being and not just their own institutional engorgement.

MAKING DISCIPLES

The commission Jesus gave us in Matthew 28 was not to "put on a good show that will bring in the multitudes." It was to "make disciples." Making disciples is a formational task. Normally we don't try to do human formation in large groups. We form adults in family-sized units, usually of under a dozen. We form citizens in classrooms of ten to thirty. We don't assume that in raising and educating children, bigger groups are better. I don't feel bad because the family down the street has ten kids and we only have three. Nobody says, "Gee, we might as well shut the Harder family down. There's only two old geezers left at home—three if you count the cat—and they haven't given birth to a new child in twenty-four years!" Nor does my wife—a schoolteacher—envy teachers who have bigger classes. She never comes home and says, "Wow—wish I had another thirty or forty kids in my class. Then I'd feel like a success as a teacher!" She knows she does her best formational work in small groups.

The same is true in forming disciples. Small groups can pay attention to the details of individual growth. Members can talk about the questions raised at work by their Muslim or Hindu colleagues. Face-to-face groups can help people wrestle through the blows to faith that sickness and death can bring. They can be accountable to and responsible for each other.

One factor that contributes to discipleship formation in smaller churches is the fact that laypeople are forced to shoulder a larger share of the ministry. As clergy climb the size ladder in their careers, they may spend little time in small places; those communities experience a fairly rapid turnover of clergy. So it falls to the laity to keep the mission going. That doesn't mean pastors aren't important. They are very useful encouragers, leaders, coaches. But the staying power is in the people. In larger churches, clergy tend to be more like managers, decision makers. People depend on them to direct the ministry. And when a pastor leaves a large church, the departure has a large impact. In smaller churches, the people make more of the decisions. One pastor in a small congregation told me that he was phoned one Saturday evening and told that there wouldn't be church the next day because a few of the council members had stained the pews and they weren't dry yet!

Listen to what Ephesians 4:11 says about the relationship between laypeople and pastors:

> [God's gifts] were that some would be apostles, some prophets, some evangelists, some pastors and teachers, *to equip the saints for the work of ministry, for building up the body of Christ, until all of us come to the unity of the faith and of the knowledge of the Son of God, to maturity, to the measure of the full stature of Christ* (italics mine).

Small places often find themselves forced to grow into "the measure of the full stature of Christ," to develop their own capacities simply because they can't afford or can't secure the services of a professional spiritual leader.

Those are some of the joys of smallness. So when I hear congregations bemoaning their shrinking size, I tell them, "You're just about small enough to be effective." And to those who have trouble believing that it's possible to be small *and* effective, I tell them (as a friend of mine says), "You haven't been in bed with a mosquito!"

Choosing to Be Small

Constantine left us a legacy of church as *grand theater,* modeled after the coliseum: many seats, all filled, gathered around a marvelous religious spectacle, led by a cadre of elite clerical performers, and flush with money. That legacy continues to be secretly treasured by most churches I've encountered. Young seminarians dream of preaching like Billy Graham or Martin Luther King Jr., attracting hundreds who will who hang on their every word. Parish councils dream of filling the pews, filling the offering plates, gaining status and respect in their community. Their secret prayer? The one Ronald McDonald has taught us: "Super size me!"

We put on "events," and when many come we inevitably say, "Now that was a success!" If the numbers are high, we rarely stop to gather any further data. Who asks, "Was the gospel actually

shared and *heard*?" "Were people's lives changed, and if so, how?"
"Does this community now reflect more clearly the character of
the life shared by Father, Son, and Spirit—and if so, in what ways?"

Perhaps it's about time we heard the people of a church that is
shrinking say, "Now, finally, we are *small enough* to be the church
Jesus intended. Small enough to know each other intimately, small
enough to share each other's stories, to pray and care for each other, to give the young, the old, the poor, and the weak a full voice
in this place, small enough to be accountable to each other and
responsible for each other. Now we are small enough that we can
work out together *in detail* what it means to be a follower of Jesus
in the grocery store, at the office, in school, in the hospital with
aging parents, or out on the tractor."

Perhaps we need a new kind of vision: many churches small
enough to build disciples well. Kennon Callahan, well-known
church leadership author, says, "The twenty-first century is the
century of small, strong congregations. More people will be drawn
to small, strong congregations than any other kind."[11] He uses the
term *strong* here not as a measure of a church's size or finances but
its engagement with its mission. In my own context, one group
of Mennonites in Alberta have chosen as their motto for all future church plants this apparent oxymoron: "small, strong, and
missional."

These folks, and many more in the small group movement that
has been active on the fringes of Canadian and American churches for decades (though also at the heart of some missionally effective large churches), know that the phrase *small is beautiful* is
not a consolation prize but an insight into the way that God often
works most effectively. Here is one final story of God's power at
work in the weak.

One Last Story

Over the course of my ministry, I have delivered many hundreds
of sermons and listened to hundreds more. I don't remember the
details of most of them. They tend to yield their nourishment and
then pass into forgetfulness, like most of our family meals. But

one is etched indelibly into my memory. It wasn't delivered by a Billy Graham or an Oswald Hoffmann. It was the simple witness of a young man with Down syndrome. That Easter season our worship team had decided to give over the sermons, at least partially, to people who weren't often heard from in the congregation. We spent time beforehand helping them to articulate their experience of God in community. "Danny" was one of them. He was a gentle fellow with a ready laugh who lived with his mother. He was active in the congregation—ushering, helping with communion, handing out bulletins, that sort of thing. But he had never spoken publicly. However, when we asked him, he agreed to share his story on a Sunday morning. He couldn't write, but he told his mother who God was in his life. He described the love that he had received from others. She wrote down his thoughts, and I helped him memorize his testimony. One Sunday morning, he stood up in front of hundreds (thousands if you include the TV broadcast), and with enormous courage slowly told his story. It was electric. The congregation was so deeply touched that almost two decades later, they still talk about it. That story of God's work from one we would regard as weak had more impact than any sermon I ever preached or heard.

If there is one thing that I value about the tools described in this book, it is that they can help to draw people like Danny into the center of church and community. They open our eyes to the possibilities for life created by Father, Son, and Holy Spirit as they clothe themselves in creation, as they put us on in all our weakness and lead us into the community-building mission of God.

Sample Appreciative Interview Questions

Appreciative inquiry is built around good questions, questions that look for what works rather than what has gone wrong, for what we value and care about rather than those things we reject, and for what we hope for rather than what we fear. Here are a few sample questions one might ask regarding a few congregational and community interests that I have selected. In each area the key thing is to focus on four types of questions:

1. What has worked well?
2. What are your core values in this area, or your congregation or community's core values?
3. What are three wishes you have for this area if you were free to hope for the best?
4. What might you be able to contribute to help one of these wishes come true?

Note: I haven't included the fourth question in every sample below, because this action-creating step is sometimes best done through another tool, such as asset mapping. This step requires a mechanism for connecting the various contributions people are willing to make into an effective, manageable project or response. That can be done through the creation of "provocative proposals" by a leadership team. But often people's ownership is increased when they generate the proposals themselves using a tool like asset mapping.

REGARDING WORSHIP

- Tell me a story about the best worship experience you have had in this parish. Describe the event in detail. What made it a memorable experience? Who was involved?
- Describe how you felt. Describe what you did as a result of the experience.
- What matters most to you in worship?
- If you could wave a magic wand making worship here the way you want it to be, what would it be like?

REGARDING COMMUNITY YOUTH

- Tell me about a time when you saw a young person making a positive difference in this community. Who was it? How did you feel? Why was what that young person did so memorable?
- What do you value about the youth in our community?
- Tell me about a time when our community did something that the youth really responded to positively. What was it? Why did they respond that way?
- Can you think of a time when you had a close relationship with a young person who was not your own family? What was it like? Why did it work?
- If you had three wishes for the youth in this community, what would they be?

REGARDING HOMELESS PEOPLE

- Tell me about a time when you saw something done by or for homeless people that had a positive impact on our community? Who did it? Why was it so valuable?
- What do you, and what does our community, value as far as housing is concerned?

- If you could have three wishes come true for the homeless in our community, what would they be?
- Is there anything you'd like to do or contribute (time, experience, personality, money, things) to help them come true?

REGARDING MINISTRY TO THE SICK

- Tell me about a time when you witnessed or experienced one of our members helping someone (yourself?) who was sick in a very effective way. What did the person do? Why was it so helpful? What was his or her relationship to the sick person?
- What do you value about our congregation or community's care for the sick?
- If you had three wishes for our congregation or community's health care, what would they be?
- What could you contribute to make your wishes a reality?

Steps in Doing a Faith-Based Appreciative Inquiry

Let your minds be filled with everything that is true, everything
that is honorable, everything that is upright and pure, everything
that we love and admire—with whatever is good and praiseworthy.
—Philippians 4:8 (New Jerusalem Bible)

STEP 1:

DEFINE THE AREA OF INTEREST OR CONCERN

A. Gather a group of eight to ten people to define the inquiry's focus. This can be done in a couple of ways, as follows:

1. *With a geographic group:* Invite articulate people from the congregation and surrounding community to discuss a question such as, "Tell us what you think are this region's greatest gifts and challenges." Such people should have experience with a fairly broad spectrum of the community (for example, social workers, chamber of commerce members, teachers, nurses, clergy, bartenders, police, addictions workers, welfare clients, and so forth). Then identify an area of interest. It might be youth or seniors' transportation, accessible worship, children's after-school care, support for those making their way through systems (health care, prison, social services), economic struggles (mine foreclosure, bankruptcy), and the like.

2. *With a social group:* If the field of interest has already been narrowed—for example, because a congregational committee already has a mandate to work with certain people—then invite folks who have a broad range of experience with that group's interest. The group might be those who have special needs, a certain age group, folks interested in housing or children's care, and so forth. Again, invite them to tell their stories about that group's gifts and challenges. Then narrow the focus to a particular issue or subinterest.

B. *Form a leadership team* to oversee the appreciative inquiry. Some of those involved in the initial discussion above might be interested.

C. *Develop questions for interviews.* These questions should be entirely positive and inquire about the following:

1. *Best Experience*—a peak time when the church or community or social group did something well in relation to the area of concern.

2. *Core Values*—what the person values most about his or her church or community or social group regarding the area of interest. How do people see themselves positively contributing to that area?

3. *Wishes*—what the person would like to see more of in the future in relation to the area of interest. What would the church or community or social group look like if those wishes came true?

4. *Commitment*—what is the person willing to offer (time, personality, things to give or lend, skills, experience, connections, and so forth) to help that wish come true? Note: This question does not have to be included in the interviews. It can be raised with the larger group during the design stage below to identify local resources and creative options for mobilizing them to help move toward the desired dream(s).

D. Make plans for how interviewers and interviewees will be recruited and how interviews will be carried out (for example, one on one or in small groups, at home or church or in the community). Fill in details for the following steps. Note: When interviews are done in pairs, rather than small groups, each interviewer should begin by interviewing another interviewer. If done in small groups, a facilitator and host is needed for each group. (The facilitator looks after group dynamics. The host sets up the space and takes notes.)

STEP 2:

DISCOVER THE LIFE-GIVING STORIES AND DYNAMIC

A. Recruit interviewers or small group facilitators and hosts.
B. Assign and prepare interviewers or facilitators and hosts. Instruct them in how to listen, record responses, and facilitate conversation. If you are using small groups, see appendix C, "Doing an Appreciative Inquiry in Small Groups: Guide for Facilitators and Hosts." Conduct one-on-one interviews or small group meetings.

STEP 3:

DREAM ABOUT POSSIBLE FUTURES

A. Leadership group (congregation and community members) gathers stories and responses from the interviewers' or facilitators' notes and identifies common themes. Themes are written up in vivid language, using the people's own phrases as much as possible.
B. Meet with a selection of those who were interviewed in the one-on-ones or small groups. Present the themes, and ask which themes hold the most promise for the church or community or social group's future.
C. Leadership group takes themes identified as most valuable and develops a small number of *provocative proposals* that describe a desired future as if it were happening already ("We value such and such, and in the next [period of time] we will do such and such"). The proposals must stretch the congregation and community, point to real,

desired possibilities, and require new learning and new relationships. Have the group vote (in the design stage) with sticky dots to reduce the options to one. This step can also be left out if an asset-mapping exercise is used in the design stage to develop the concrete proposals.

STEP 4:
DESIGN

A. Hold a large gathering in order to meet with as many as possible of those in the church or community or social group. The design stage can be done in a couple of ways:
    1. Present the dreams, choose one of them (participants can vote using sticky dots on newsprint sheets that describe each idea), and then do an asset-mapping exercise to develop and select concrete proposals.
    2. In a larger congregation or agency, present all the provocative proposals, and ask participants for feedback as to how the proposals would affect various groups, ministries, and organizations in the community and congregation.
B. While the large group is gathered, identify formal and informal groups that may be interested in helping to make the provocative proposal(s) happen. Set a date and place for initial meetings. Take down the names and contact information for those who will be involved in the action.
C. Before leaving, ask the large group to brainstorm a covenant that outlines their concrete commitments to make their vision a reality. Post it somewhere visible in the church and community.

STEP 5:
DELIVER

Make sure that action groups meet and act on their commitments. Too many great ideas end up collecting dust on a shelf.

For more information on using appreciative inquiry in ministry, see the following:

- The Clergy Leadership Institute (www.clergyleadership. com). Rev. Dr. Rob Voyle leads this center that trains clergy in appreciative inquiry techniques for a variety of settings.
- "Get Fit, Keep Fit: Covenant in Minstry" of the Anglican Church Diocese of Vancouver toolkit for using an appreciative inquiry in a congregational setting: www. vancouver.anglican.ca/OurMinistry/SupportingParishes/ GetFitKeepFit.aspx.
- Mark Lau Branson, *Memories, Hopes, and Conversations: Appreciative Inquiry and Congregational Change* (Herndon: VA: Alban Institute, 2004).

Doing an Appreciative Inquiry in Small Groups

Guide for Facilitators and Hosts

Group Facilitator's Responsibilities

For *each* gathering that the facilitator plans to lead, he or she

1. Recruits a host (see responsibilities below).
2. Invites and receives positive responses from four to six people (besides the facilitator and the host) who are willing to attend the inquiry.
3. Leads the small group discussion, focusing on the appreciative inquiry questions, making sure that everyone has adequate input.
4. After the small group gathering, together with the host, summarizes the notes taken by the host, using the "Facilitator's Form for Summarizing Responses" below.
5. Submits the summary to the Appreciative Inquiry Leadership Team by _____. The committee will collate and present some action ideas (provocative propositions) at a closing potluck, where those attending will decide on a direction to take.

Host's Responsibilities

1. Offers a space in his or her home for a gathering of six to eight people, or prepares space in another place (church, school, or some other public space).
2. Provides simple refreshments.
3. Takes notes on people's responses during the gathering, using the "Host's Form for Taking Notes" below.
4. Helps the facilitator interpret the notes so that the facilitator can create a summary of people's responses.

Agenda for an Appreciative Inquiry Small Group Gathering

1. Welcome people as they arrive; offer a light refreshment.
2. Arrange chairs in a circle. Ask participants to share names, year each person first attended this church (or entered the geographic area or the social group that is the focus of the inquiry), and then briefly why they became part of this area or group.
3. Explain the purpose of the gathering—to identify our strengths, core values, and dreams so that we can begin to build on them. Say a little about the nature of an appreciative inquiry (drawing loosely on the material in appendix B as appropriate). Say, "This is not a time for complaints. We begin assuming that we are sinners and that [our region or social group] is not perfect. We also begin assuming that *God* is at work here. We could spend our time picking out the faults. But that would just make us experts on the problems. We'd rather focus on what God is up to and join in with God to build a stronger community among the folks [in our region or social group]." *Emphasize the great value of each person's perspective and experience.*
4. Go through the appreciative inquiry questions that the leadership team has developed. Allow (don't force) each

person to respond to the first question before going on to the second, and so on.

- Say, "To make sure that all, even the quieter ones, get a chance to tell their stories, I'll keep an eye on the time and signal when it's time for each person to wrap it up." (For a signal, the facilitator could quietly but visibly lay a brightly colored card or piece of paper on the table.)

- Say, "Please give as much detail as you can within your time. We want to know *what* is important and valuable to you about [area of interest], and *why*. We are especially interested in your stories—particular incidents, situations. Try to speak to your own experience rather than generalizing." The facilitator should have a list of subquestions from the appreciative inquiry leadership team to prompt group members if they are too general or have time left they haven't used.

- At the beginning of a round, give the whole group about a minute to think of their response before the first one starts so that they can listen completely to each other and not be thinking up their own response. The facilitator should probably begin the first round (with his or her own response to the question) and then allow someone else to begin subsequent rounds.

- After each has shared, say, "Thank you, [John, Mary, and so on]," but don't comment. Then go on to the next person.

5. At the end of the third round, you might close in prayer, thanking God for some of the ways God has been at work, as revealed in the stories told by the group. If the entire group is Christian, you might consider inviting group members to offer one-sentence prayers in this form: "Thank you, God, for [such and such] that you did for me or us [around the area of interest]."

6. Debrief: Ask for a few responses to questions such as,
   "What was this experience like for you? What happened to
   the energy in the group? What happened to your feelings
   about [the area of interest]?"

Things to Remember and Take Note Of

- *Focus on the positive.* This is not a time for complaining
  about programs, buildings, or the pastor or other leaders.
  If people begin to do that, say something like, "Jane, you're
  right—like any [church or community or social group]
  there's lots that could be improved. The reason we are
  gathering today is to help make those improvements by
  focusing on what *God* is up to, not on what sin or the devil
  are doing. We want to know what we do well, and care
  about most, and to build on that. Today we want to be
  experts on the solutions, not on the problems." Emphasize
  that this doesn't mean suppressing complaints or denying
  problems. It simply means that the *first* thing we want to
  see is God's activity.
- *Help people to share their stories without evaluation or
  interruption.* Say to the group, "We'll let each person tell
  his or her story within the alloted time. You might ask a
  question for more detail if there's time at the end. But we'll
  try to let each person tell his or her experience without
  commenting on it."

APPRECIATIVE INQUIRY FACILITATOR'S FORM FOR SUMMARIZING RESPONSES

This form should be written up, in conversation with the host,
within twenty-four hours of the gathering, while memories are
fresh. Look not only for similarities among responses but also for
opposites or unusual responses that may indicate a resource or
perspective that has been overlooked. Try to use participants' own
language as much as possible.

Question 1: Best Experiences

If the area of interest has not been determined, ask yourself, "In listening to participants, what areas of the church's or community's life did peak experiences tend to occur in? What was happening in those area(s) that people cared about?" If the area of interest has been narrowed, ask, "What was it in our community's work (with youth, for example) that people feel really good about? Which stories really stood out and why? What worked and why?"

Question 2: Core Values

In listening to participants, are there clusters of core values around our area of interest that might be grouped under one or two general headings? What would those headings be? Give a couple of vivid illustrations of the core value(s) that surfaced most often.

Question 3: Dreams

In listening to participants, what are some of the dreams they have for our area of interest? Why do they hope for those things? To what extent do their dreams build on best experiences, as opposed to filling in what is missing? In what ways did they talk about how their dreams could be realized by extending or developing areas of best experience or core values?

APPRECIATIVE INQUIRY HOST'S FORM FOR TAKING NOTES

Number of people participating (guess ages)
Early years (under 30): _____
Middle years (31–55): _____
Later years (over 56): _____

Host: _____
Facilitator: _____
Date: _____

Record a vivid phrase or sentence or two, in the participant's own words, from each person who speaks to each question. Try to capture the heart of the story or value or dream that the person is describing. But don't worry about getting too many details. The overall picture is what we will ultimately be looking for.

You will probably do best if you use a separate sheet of paper to record each group member's responses to each of the following questions. (The facilitator will have the exact questions.)

Question 1: Best experience or highlight
Question 2: Core values—what we care most about
Question 3: Dreams for the future

THEOLOGY AND THEORY BEHIND APPRECIATIVE INQUIRY

This information can be used with the steering committee as a way of preparing for the appreciative inquiry and as an introduction to the participants in the storytelling phase.

What causes an organization to change? Generally, change requires one of two things—a deep, immediate, emergent threat to its own survival, or a vision of a new future for the organization that is attractive and realizable, combined with an infusion of new energy and resources. Essentially, change is caused by *fear* and by *hope*.

We might call this law and gospel. Law is that experience we all have when we feel that we ought to be more than we are. It's that sense that something important in our lives is seriously at risk. Law essentially operates on the basis of fear. It's a deep awareness of what will happen if we don't take some action or if we take the wrong action.

In many churches, change is driven by fear. "We're losing our young people; we don't have enough money to maintain our ministry"; and so on. Fear can work, to some extent, and it is sometimes necessary to wake us up. It can be the work of God's Spirit—as we often see in the prophets. But the downside is that it tends to make us focus on our shortcomings. We start the blame game.

We can become experts on the problem, without being any closer to solutions.

Hope is the other change agent, and it is more powerful. Hope comes out of an experience of the gospel. Hope comes when we discover that God is at work among us, doing wonderful things—that God has hidden resources and possibilities in our community that we didn't know existed—like buried treasure. Hope emerges when we realize that by the grace of God our future is not determined by past problems or social movements or economic trends. Rather, our future belongs to God—to the one who holds the power of a billion galaxies in his hand and for whom the past and the present are no obstacle to the future.

We arouse hope with these three questions: (1) What has God been up to among us? (2) What then matters the most? What is God's style, God's focus? (3) What possibilities does that open up for us in the future? Appreciative inquiry focuses on what God is doing, not on what sin and the devil are doing. We want to be experts first on what God is up to.

Another theological assumption is that, ultimately, God's mission in this world is to build community that reflects the kind of community that exists inside God, in the Trinity. A wonderfully open giving and receiving, challenging, affirming, equipping, and sharing happens between the Father, Son, and Holy Spirit. God wants to create a reflection of that in our congregation and community.

As we gather to share in this group our best experiences, our hopes and deep values, we are already building community. This is already a small fulfillment of the mission of God. We share here a small piece of God's life. So an appreciative inquiry is not just about creating new ministries or starting programs. It's also about connecting you to each other and to God.

Finally, here are *a few theoretical assumptions* that are embedded in this process. They're based on how human beings work—our psychology and group dynamics:

1. *What we focus on becomes our reality.* If we see ourselves as a problem institution, we'll be one. If we see ourselves

as an institution that works, then we'll become an institution that works. Recognizing that truth does not mean
denying the problems. It simply means that we first look
for what is good, what works, and focus on it.

2. *The questions we ask determine our focus.* If we ask,
    "What's wrong with this place?" we'll see it as a place that
    is wrong. If we ask, "What's right with this place?" we'll
    see it as a place that is right. The language we use matters a
    lot.

3. *Like plants, people tend to grow toward the light.* Hope is
    a better long-term motivator than fear. Fear tends to be
    quite short term. Hope draws us toward the things that
    satisfy us, that make life whole and good. Fear simply
    drives us away from the things that dissatisfy and hurt us.
    Once we've got a little distance, we stop moving. It's short
    term. It gives us nothing more than neutrality and doesn't
    bring life that is fulfilling.

4. *To move into the future with confidence we need to take the
    best out of our past.* So we have to find out what that is.

5. *We have to work together.* No leader alone knows what is
    best for a community. No individual can bring positive
    change by herself. Each of us has to tell our story of what
    has worked, what matters most, what we hope for, if the
    full resources of this congregation are to be uncovered.

Notes

Preface

1. Philadelphia: Division for Parish Services, Lutheran Church in America, 1986.
2. Gregory Pierce, *Of Human Hands: A Reader in the Spirituality of Work* (Minneapolis: Augsburg, 1991), 24ff. See also Pierce's reflections on finding the sacred in the ordinary, 16–24.
3. See, for example, University of Maryland professor Carol Graham's *The Pursuit of Happiness: An Economy of Well-Being* (Washington, DC: Brookings Institution Press, 2011).

Chapter 1: The Church's Community-Building Mission

1. See, for example, his book *Education for Critical Consciousness* (New York: Continuum, 2005), or *The Pedagogy of the Oppressed* (New York: Continuum, 2000).
2. "The Trillions of Microbes That Call Us Home—and Help Keep Us Healthy," *Discover*, March 2011, http://discovermagazine.com/2011/mar/04-trillions-microbes-call-us-home-help-keep-healthy.
3. For example, Jürgen Moltmann has a strong critique of what he calls "monarchic monotheism" in *The Crucified God: The Cross of Christ as the Foundation and Criticism of Christian Theology*, trans. R. A. Wilson and John Bowden (London: SCM Press, 1974), 326.
4. Peter Miller, "The Genius of Swarms," *National Geographic*, July 2007, http://ngm.nationalgeographic.com/print/2007/07/swarms/miller-text.
5. *Anglican Theological Review* 83, no. 2 (Spring 2001): 239–54.
6. *God and Human Suffering: An Exercise in the Theology of the Cross* (Philadelphia: Fortress Press, 1987).

Chapter 2: Public Church

1. Paraphrased without citation in Randall Sorenson, *Minding Spirituality*, Relational Perspective Book Series (London: Routledge, 2004), 153.
2. *Democracy and Tradition* (Princeton, NJ: Princeton University Press, 2005).
3. For extended discussions see Ulrich Duchrow, *Two Kingdoms: The Use and Misuse of a Lutheran Theological Concept* (Geneva, Switzerland: Lutheran World Federation, Department of Studies, 1977), or Gordon Jensen, "The Significance of Luther's Theology of the Cross for Contemporary Political and Contextual Theologies" (Ph.D. diss., University of St. Michael's College, 1992).
4. The law is also used spiritually to convict of sin, but in this discussion our primary interest is in its civil use.
5. *Luther's Works,* American ed., gen ed. Jaroslav Pelikan and Helmut T. Lehmann (St. Louis: Concordia Publishing House, and Philadelphia: Fortress Press, 1955–86), 13:195. See also 13:196.
6. For more on this, see James Cook, *Community Development Theory* (University of Missouri Extension, Dept. of Community Development, 1994), http://extension.missouri.edu/publications/DisplayPub.aspx?P=MP568.
7. For a wonderful treatment of how *perichosis*—the deep indwelling of the persons of the Trinity—means that Father, Son, and Spirit choose to share each other's suffering, see Jürgen Moltmann, *The Crucified God: The Cross of Christ as the Foundation and Criticism of Christian Theology*, trans. R. A. Wilson and John Bowden (London: SCM Press, 1974), 83.
8. *An Unstoppable Force: Daring to Become the Church God Had in Mind* (Loveland, CO: Group Publishing, 2001), 23.
9. John Haught, *Christianity and Science: Toward a Theology of Nature* (Maryknoll, NY: Orbis, 2007).
10. See "Social Inclusion and Community Economic Development," August 2006, http://www.ccednet-rcdec.ca/files/ccednet/PCCDLN_Final_Report.pdf.
11. For a provocative exploration of the political implications of Jesus's parables, see William Herzog, *The Parables of Jesus as Subversive Speech: Jesus as Pedagogue of the Oppressed* (Louisville, KY: Westminster John Knox Press, 1994).
12. *Binding the Strong Man: A Political Reading of Mark's Story of Jesus,* 2nd ed. (New York: Maryknoll, 2008).
13. See the summary by Daniel Schwartz, "Volunteering in Numbers," *The National*, February 4, 2002, http://www.cbc.ca/news/bigpicture/volunteer/volunteering.html.

Chapter 3: Appreciative Inquiry

1. *The Social Construction of Reality: A Treatise in the Sociology of Knowledge* (New York: Anchor, 1967).
2. *Hope within History* (Louisville, KY: Westminster John Knox Press, 1987), 85.
3. *Letters and Papers from Prison* (New York: Touchstone, 1997), 17.
4. John Haught, *Christianity and Science: Toward a Theology of Nature* (Maryknoll, NY: Orbis, 2007).
5. See David Cooperrider, Peter Sorenson Jr., Diana Whitney, and Therese Yaeger, *Appreciative Inquiry: Rethinking Human Organization toward a Positive Theory of Change* (Champaign, IL: Stipes, 1999); David Cooperrider and Suresh Srivastva, *Appreciative Management and Leadership: The Power of Positive Thought and Action in Organization* (Brunswick, OH: Crown Custom Publishing, 1999). A number of books have since been published by Cooperrider, Srivastva, and colleagues on appreciative inquiry.
6. Mark Branson, in his book *Memories, Hopes, and Conversations: Appreciative Inquiry and Congregational Change* (Herndon VA: Alban Institute, 2004), 139–40, gives an excellent, detailed report on how the process can be used in a congregation's life and mission.
7. Bertrand Russell, *Mysticism and Logic and Other Essays* (1918; repr. Totowa, NJ: Barnes and Noble Books, 1981), 47.
8. I am indebted to the "Get Fit, Keep Fit" program of the Anglican Church of Canada, Diocese of New Westminster, for some of the language in this outline of assumptions. See http://www.vancouver.anglican.ca/Portals/0/GetFit/PDF%20files/Appreciative%20Inquiry%20&%20the%20Church.pdf.
9. For example, see Bill O'Hanlon and Michele Weiner-Davis, *In Search of Solutions* (New York: Norton, 1989), as an early example of solution-focused therapy.
10. For example, the Canadian government's public health agency's effort to identify individual behaviors or patterns of behavior that lead to better health. See its website, http://cbpp-pcpe.phac-aspc.gc.ca/.
11. For example, J. Sternin and R. Pascale, "Your Company's Secret Change Agents," *Harvard Business Review*, May 2005, or Dennis Sparks, "Principals Amplifying Teachers' Outstanding Practices," *Results*, May 2005.
12. See *Building Strategic Partnerships to Foster Inclusion*, Corporation for National and Community Service, 2003, www.serviceandinclusion.org.
13. Note at this point the intern narrowed the possibilities for spiritual expression to that of worship. It might have been better to still keep it open-ended.
14. See "Get Fit, Keep Fit."

Chapter 4: Asset Mapping

1. Term coined by Arien Mack and Irvin Rock, *Inattentional Blindness* (Cambridge, MA: MIT Press, 2000).
2. "Test Your Awareness: Do the Test," YouTube, http://www.youtube.com/watch?v=Ahg6qcgoay4.
3. For a fuller discussion of the effect of this trait on group decision making, see Jon Jenkins and Maureen Jenkins, *The 9 Disciplines of a Facilitator: Leading Groups by Transforming Yourself* (San Francisco: Jossey-Bass, 2006), 90–91.
4. See www.luthersnow.com for a list of resources and consulting expertise.
5. Ibid.
6. James B. Cook, "Community Development Theory," University of Missouri Extension, October 1994, pub. no. MP568; online, April 2010, http://extension.missouri.edu/publications/DisplayPub.aspx?P=MP568.
7. *The Journal of Bone and Joint Surgery* (American volume) 81, no. 9 (Sept. 1999): 1205.
8. Scientists such as Andreas Albrecht and Stuart Kauffman suggest that even the physical laws that we take for granted may be changing. These laws have been understood to govern the relationships between elements in our universe. And many physicists have searched hard for the one law, or "theory of everything," that explains it all. But Albrecht, Kauffman, and others suggest that in a dynamic, evolving universe, that sort of approach is unhelpfully reductionist. Just as the relationships between entities in our universe change, these scientists suggest that the basic principles on which they are built may also be evolving. See "Who Wrote the Book of Physics?" *Discover*, April 2010, 32–37.
9. Terry Fretheim does some wonderful work with these concepts in *God and World in the Old Testament: A Relational Theology of Creation* (Nashville: Abingdon Press, 2005).
10. See Zeeya Merali, "Back from the Future," *Discover*, April 2010, 38–44 (42).
11. See *Building Resilience in Rural Communities: Toolkit* (Toowoomba, Queensland: University of Queensland and University of Southern Queensland, 2008), http://learningforsustainability.net/pubs/Building%20Resilience%20in%20Rural%20Communities%20Toolkit.pdf.

Chapter 5: Beyond Strength

1. See Robert Kelly in *Theologia Crucis*, unpublished 2001 lecture notes, Waterloo Lutheran Seminary, 103–5, 118–20.
2. See Ched Myer's ground-breaking commentary *Binding the Strongman: A Political Reading of Mark's Story of Jesus* (New York: Orbis, 1988) for a

wonderful socioliterary investigation of the way in which Jesus challenges the power of Rome and the temple trade. Chapter 5 on the demon-possessed pigs, chapter 11 on the cursing of the fig tree, and chapter 12 on the question of paying taxes to Caesar are particularly revealing of the way in which we have interpreted biblical stories to avoid their empire-challenging character.

3. Minneapolis: Fortress Press, 2005, 171.

4. For a thorough treatment, see John Ralston Saul, *A Fair Country* (Toronto, ON: Viking Canada, 2008).

5. *Images of the Church in the New Testament.* In publication since 1960. A recent edition was published by Westminster John Knox Press in 2005.

6. See James B. Davies, Susanna Sandström, Anthony Shorrocks, and Edward N. Wolff in "The World Distribution of Household Wealth," Discussion Paper No. 2008/03, United Nations University, World Institute for Development Economics Research (Helsinki: UNU-WIDER, 2008), 22, http://www.wider.unu.edu/publications. See also the press release at www.wider.unu.edu/events/past-events/2006-events/en_GB/05-12-2006/.

7. See, for example, the *Saskatchewan Rural Youth Healthy Lifestyles and Risk Behaviour Project,* Rural, Remote and Northern Women's Health, Prairie Women's Health Centre of Excellence, http://www.pwhce.ca/program_rural_youth.htm, especially the fact sheet on alcoholism at http://www.pwhce.ca/pdf/youth/Fact_Sheet7Alcohol.pdf. According to the Royal Canadian Mounted Police, traffic deaths are the leading cause of death and injury among Canada's young people, and more than 80 percent of those deaths take place in rural areas. See RCMP *Road Safety Vision 2010,* http://www.rcmp-grc.gc.ca/ts-sr/prog-eng.htm.

8. *The Church in the Power of the Spirit: A Contribution to Messianic Ecclesiology* (Minneapolis: Fortress Press, 1993), 129.

9. I explore some of these in my doctoral dissertation, *The Shame of Farm Bankruptcy: A Sociological and Theological Investigation of Its Effect on Rural Communities,* http://cameronharder.com/publications_presentations/index.htm.

10. See for example *The Multi-Grade Classroom: Myth and Reality—A Canadian Study*, ed. Margaret Gayfer, extracted from research by Joel Gajadharsingh (Toronto: Christian Education Association, 1991).

11. Kennon Callahan, *Small, Strong Congregations: Creating Strengths and Health for Your Congregation* (San Francisco: Jossey-Bass, 2000), 12–13.